Table of Contents

Desperate Times. Desperate Measures.

Editor's Note

This book is not only a collection of essays and stories by a bunch of funny, talented, smart writers, it is also a vote for a certain way of life. The bookish life. More specifically, the bookstore life.

It is published in support of Independent Bookstore Day, and each of the writers herein donated their work to the cause. But the cause is not simply our one-day celebration of independent bookstores, the cause is what those bookstores represent—and there are 1,664 in the U.S, sprinkled across all fifty states.

Independent bookstores are not just stores, they're community centers and local anchors run by passionate readers.

They are entire universes of ideas that contain the possibility of real serendipity. They are lively performance spaces and quiet places where aimless perusal is a day well spent.

Indie bookstores, whether dusty and labyrinthine or clean and well-lit, are not just stores, they are solutions. They hold the key to your love life, your career, and your passions. Walking the aisles of a good bookstore means stumbling upon a novel that expands your heart. It's encountering an art book that changes the direction of your life. It's the joy of having a perfect stranger steer you toward the perfect book.

In a world of tweets and algorithms and pageless digital downloads, bookstores are not a dying anachronism. They are living, breathing organisms that continue to grow and expand. In fact, there are more of them this year than there were last year, and there were more last year than the year before. Horror stories like James Patterson's aside, indie bookstores aren't going anywhere.

What the twenty-one pieces in this book offer, along with entertainment, laughter, and that deeply felt zing of recognition that good writing provides, are twenty-one rousing cheers for the importance of bookstores in our collective lives. And for that we are profoundly grateful.

—Samantha Schoech, May 2015

Bad Bosses, Horrible Jobs, and Awful Coworkers

Haterade

By Meghan Daum

When I was twenty-five years old I appeared in the pages
of the *New York Times Magazine* in my underwear. Well,
almost. A cartoon drawing of a girl in her underwear—a
girl who, with her short blond hair and apple cheeks over
a pointed chin, looked remarkably like me—appeared
in conjunction with an essay I'd written about the way
Generation X was reacting to the safe-sex message. The year
was 1996 and the AIDS crisis, though technically past its
apogee, seemed to have finally succeeded in infiltrating every
corner of the general public consciousness and scaring the
hell out of it. Invitations to get tested for HIV loomed from
billboards and in subway ads. Celebrities preached about

safer sex in public-service announcements. Music videos and advertisements appropriated AIDS awareness as not only a form of provocation but an agent of style. It was the year of the Broadway debut of *Rent*, a modern-day retelling of *La Bohème* that featured several characters who were either infected with HIV or dying of AIDS.

The essay had been brewing in my mind since at least two years before, when I'd been jolted by a print advertisement for the Benetton clothing company. It featured more than a thousand tiny photos of smiling, attractive young people purporting to represent every part of the world. Intermittent faces were shaded and partially obscured by the word *AIDS*, creating a visual effect that spelled out the word in larger type when you looked at the image from farther back. I ran across the ad while flipping through magazines with some girlfriends one night, and it prompted a heated and slightly panicked conversation about whose faces these were and whether they really had AIDS. One friend said, "Yes, of course they do; that's how bad things have gotten." Another wasn't sure, and I thought it couldn't be possible. This led to an even more heated discussion about how dangerous the world was and how we, as twenty-something females living in New York City, should perhaps hang up our dancing shoes (or, in our case, black leather lace-up boots) and marry the next person we met (after the requisite health screenings, of course), lest the single life literally kill us.

I was a young writer back then. I won't say "aspiring writer," because I'd actually managed to publish a few things that elevated me slightly out of the "aspiring" camp and were steering me into the "promising" camp. Still, I was green. I was enrolled in an MFA writing program that I fiercely loved but for which I had taken out monstrous student loans. It seemed worth it, though. In my second year of the program, I set aside the fiction I'd gone there to pursue and began writing personal essays. Things started clicking almost immediately and a central theme emerged: the relationship between myself and society, the tension between the trappings of contemporary life and its actualities, what it meant to be "alive" (i.e., twenty-five years old) in "today's world" (i.e., New York City). And, as is always the case for a young writer, every experience I had—every book I read and film I saw, every trip to the corner deli, every ranter I heard in the street—was potential fodder for another piece of groundbreaking, human condition–explaining nonfiction.

Hence the week in the fall of 1995 when, after visiting the health-services office of my university for a head cold and

new to say about my generation, I sent him the AIDS essay and he immediately invited me to lunch to discuss it further. Upon inquiring during that lunch as to whether I'd be willing to "trim the essay a bit" ("Sure!" I chirped. "Anything you want!"), another lunch was scheduled, this time at Orso with two more editors who plied me with yellow fin tuna and told me the piece would need to be cut nearly in half to accommodate a two-page spread, but that I shouldn't worry because I was the voice of my generation and everything would be spectacular.

They were right about the spectacle. Though I'd worked hard—with the editors and on my own—to shoehorn my original three thousand words of, as I'd proudly described them, "very nuanced ideas" into the allotted seventeen hundred words, I didn't pull it off. The final edit was abrupt, not all that coherent, gratuitously provocative, and suggested that I might have had unprotected sex with upward of five hundred people (in truth, the number was in the low single digits, and "unprotected" was a matter of interpretation). In addition to the tarty cartoon drawing (which had been sent to press without my knowledge, and which the art department had conceded to only after I declined to sit for a photo shoot), the essay had been assigned the awkward title of "Safe-Sex

Lies." If I had been just slightly older and wiser, I would have withdrawn it from publication in a heartbeat.

But of course I was neither of those things. I was the voice of my generation, which, in the case of this article, wasn't proving to be a very appealing one. The article came out, the *Times* received roughly six hundred irate letters within five days, my phone rang off the hook, and I was invited to appear on the NBC *Nightly News*. Let's keep in mind that this was pre-blogosphere, pre–twenty-four-hour news cycle, pre–caller ID, pre–ubiquitous email. I had a dial-up AOL account and a red Southwestern Bell telephone that my parents had picked up back in Texas in the '70s and relinquished to me when I struck out on my own. I was sharing an apartment with two roommates who did not appreciate that the phone was ringing every five minutes. Usually the person on the other end had called to say how disgusted they were with what I'd written and what a slut I was and how I was either appallingly homophobic (for suggesting that HIV might not be affecting heterosexuals at the same rate) or had a "pro-gay agenda" (for suggesting HIV was a problem at all). My classmates, who'd been the first to read the piece back in workshop, seemed perturbed about the whole thing. (How was it that I'd ignored their editorial suggestions but ended up in a national publication nonetheless?) My parents were rightfully mortified, and my friends were rapidly growing tired of talking me off a cliff every day, listening to my whining and rationalizations, and telling me what I wanted to hear, which is that the "right people" understood what I was trying to get across; I was ahead of my time; and, besides, no one was saying I was a bad writer, merely a bad person.

When a correspondent for the NBC *Nightly News* came to interview me in my apartment (roommates eavesdropping from the kitchen as they made grilled cheese sandwiches), I tried to acquit myself but mostly made things worse by rambling on in a sound bite–unfriendly fashion (again with the "dystopia") and looking slightly derelict with an aggressively short, bleached-blond haircut (it was the mid-'90s, after all). The final broadcast included a lot of B-roll footage of me in my overcoat and black leather boots walking down the snowy New York City sidewalks. When the segment ended and Tom Brokaw looked up from his desk monitor and into the camera, he shook his head with an air of such profound, almost avuncular concern that I felt like I had been sent to my room. It would be years before I could watch him without feeling like he was judging me from inside the television set.

Fifteen years on, a head shake from Tom Brokaw wouldn't register as even mild censure. As much as the culture has eased up on HIV-preventative scare tactics, it's become ruthlessly punitive in the face of just about any point of view that embraces ambiguity or gets expressed in a less-than-literal fashion. A young person (any person) who published a piece as incendiary as "Safe-Sex Lies" today would be chewed up and spit out so many times over by bloggers and commenters and cable-news screamers that the idea of "understanding what I was trying to get across" would seem not just quaint but moot. Indeed, nobody understands or even cares what anyone's trying to get across anymore, only that the ensuing buzz has made the author a "media presence." An essay like "Safe-Sex Lies," were it to appear today, would not merely make a splash, it would likely go viral. It would ricochet around email boxes, fill those yawning expanses of airtime on talk radio, and appear on the home pages of countless news aggregators, all the while dragging behind it an ever-expanding trail of "response," much of it from people who haven't read all, or perhaps any, of the essay, but nonetheless feel compelled to weigh in. The writer would then be inveighed upon to react to the reaction, to compose blog posts and participate in live chat sessions and call in to radio programs, not so much in an attempt to clarify the original message, but to talk about how "interesting" the public reception has been, and what a "wild ride" it all is—"wild ride" being a euphemism for thousands of anonymous internet comments calling you unprintable words.

These days, being attacked isn't just the result of saying something badly, it's the result of saying anything at all. I can testify to this, because for nearly ten years, I have been a weekly opinion columnist for the *Los Angeles Times*. This is a great gig, and I have many loyal, smart, thoughtful readers. But I also live with the fact that practically everything I write is met with an avalanche of invective. It runs the gamut from partisan attacks to personal attacks to entreaties to my editors to stop publishing me immediately. Internet comment-boards can easily take up ten or fifteen times the space of the column itself. My email in-box overflows with outrage and umbrage: "Shame on you!" "You are an idiot and a disgrace." "What a stupid little twit you are." And, in one of my recent favorites, "You have no credibility because you let your opinion get in the way."

Some weeks, if I've hit a particularly sensitive nerve, blogs of every imaginable variety will link to the column, offer their own spin, and then invite their own legions to chime in. On one hand, of course, this is what every columnist wants most. Like anyone who publicly expresses his ideas, be it through writing or music or visual media or anything else, the goal is to be heard, to inspire reaction and generate discussion. But based on much of the reaction I get—especially the comments in my own paper, where a stable of regulars have become so personally invested in their dislike for me that they've taken to remarking not on my column but on my looks, marital or reproductive status, and standing on the bitch-o-meter—I can hardly give myself credit for starting anything resembling a discussion. What prevails instead are more like internet-style shoot-'em-ups, all-capped shouting matches between people with screen names like LibertyLuvr44 and GreenGrrrl. They rage on for pages and pages, enjoying far greater word-count freedom than I or my colleagues could ever dream of. Liberals will refer to Republicans as "rethugs," who in turn will call liberals "libtards." Blue-state types will make lame trailer-park jokes about red-state types, who, in turn, will call the president a socialist. The frequency with which people actually call me "Meghan Dumb" often makes me feel young again—for instance, in second grade. My commenters also have a great affinity for making things up—again, a freedom not enjoyed by those in the newsroom.

"Meghan is 40 years old and still not married. Tick tock tick tock... Anyone who knows Meghan knows of what I speak. She's an angry middle aged woman and an intolerant hack."

"What a pathetic, inept, and uninformed person you are. Your articles are brainless, and when I read them I think of how miserable as a person you must be. Probably a fat ugly little girl who needs to prey on others to feel better...A fat, ugly squashed bug."

"You are a vile, loathsome, despicable pig. Your stench permeates through the web."

Let me make one thing perfectly clear. I know that online hecklers represent but a tiny fraction of readers. I also know it's actually a privilege to get feedback like this. It means that people are actually reading what I write, that editors are actually publishing it, and, moreover, that I've been able to make a career out of observing the culture and expressing my thoughts in writing. Over the years, I've scrambled to pay rent with enough menial office jobs to know better than to take even one day of uninterrupted, paid (or even unpaid) writing for granted. I know that a lot of writers would kill to be called a squashed bug or a despicable pig, if only because it beats not being called anything at all. But if most writers have long understood that publishing is a privilege that carries certain responsibilities—foremost among them taking the time to present ideas in a careful and thoughtful manner, ideally with the help of one or more editors—many readers seem to be approaching their commenting privileges like teenagers with newly minted driver's licenses. Belted in by anonymity and often distracted by the equally reckless ravings of their peers, they take potshots, spread untruths, and, at their worst, spew racism and bigotry that would put a professional writer out of business in a nanosecond. In so doing, they spread a rancor that can eclipse not only the original article but also the comments of readers who take a more constructive, civil approach. They take the very privilege the internet has afforded all of us—the privilege of equal opportunity, instant expression—and spit on it, making the very notion of "speaking your mind" seem almost like a dirty practice, the national pastime of the lowest common denominator.

This "haterade" (as the young blogger types have brilliantly coined it) is especially acute around political subjects and, in the case of my colleagues and myself, doubly acute when it comes to President Obama or Hillary Clinton or Sarah Palin or any subject remotely connected to race or gender. It by no means stops there, though. I've written about everything from shelter pets to the lost pleasures of waiting for the mail, and still been called a "retarded scum pile that personifys [*sic*] everything that's wrong with society today." As many times as I've been called a feminazi—more than once by Rush Limbaugh, who apparently skims my column regularly—I've had liberals calling for my resignation because I'm not politically correct enough, and feminists wanting to break my knees over any number of perceived slights to the cause. Like most of my fellow columnists, I'm told on a daily basis that I'm utterly unqualified for my job and the sole reason that print media is dying. For all the sputtering outrage I've provoked in my socially conservative readers—most of whom know nothing about me but nonetheless like to fantasize that I'm some kind of East Coast blue blood who gets abortions in her spare time and was educated entirely by vegetarian, Marxist lesbians at fancy schools I didn't have to pay for ("Meghan comes from a very rich family that paid for all her schooling and supported her lavish lifestyle," a commenter once declared)—I also hear from plenty of humorless progressive types who find me "offensive" and "terribly disappointing," and who want to be removed from my mailing list immediately.

Admittedly, I'm the kind of person who's capable of hearing a single boo amid a cascade of applause. Though I don't always realize it, a lot of the feedback is not only positive and flattering, but critical in ways that I need to hear and fully accept. (One of the great lessons of doing a weekly column is accepting that you won't hit it out of the park every single week and that your audience has a right to inform you when those weeks occur.) Though I know that it would be a lot better for everyone (first and foremost my husband, who must endure my efforts to "reappropriate" the meanness by printing out the most egregious examples and attaching them to the refrigerator) if I could just focus on the respectful communiqués, it's not always easy. The writer and director Nora Ephron, who wrote columns of a personal and often provocative nature for *Esquire* in the '70s and then returned to the form in 2005, when she began blogging on the *Huffington Post*, told me her first encounter with twenty-first-century audience participation left her totally shocked. "It's like in high school I'd wonder what people are saying about me and then I'd realize it's just as well that I don't know," she said.

In "The Readers Strike Back," a particularly thoughtful article on this subject that appeared on *Salon* back in 2007 (*Salon* being famous for some of the more affronted and pious commenters on the web), Gary Kamiya admitted that "it's very hard for writers, who want to be read and want to know what readers are saying about them, to ignore letters or blogs about themselves." He quoted *Salon* senior writer Laura Miller, who allowed that "practically every writer I know has gone through the mill with this," and then invoked Anthony Trollope's line from *Phineas Finn:* "But who is there that abstains from reading that which is printed in abuse of himself?'"

Though I've never been tempted to go undercover to avenge myself, as was the case with Lee Siegel, the *New Republic* reporter who created a false account and attacked his attackers on his blog on the magazine's website (and got himself suspended in the process), I do have my share of confrontation fantasies. I've often imagined tracking down some of my more vehement detractors, knocking on their doors and asking, "Who are you? What has made you so angry? What has happened in your life that you're reduced to spewing bile at people you know nothing about?"

It turns out I'm not the only one with this fantasy. Last year's short-lived reality show, succinctly entitled *H8R* (if you can't decipher that idiom, you are too old to be watching the program), followed celebrities like Snooki and Kim Kardashian as they confronted people who'd said mean things about them on the internet. It would be foolish, of course, to expect a show of this kind to offer anything terribly insightful about this phenomenon. Since the haters weren't hiding behind screen names but instead proclaiming their hate on camera and keeping it in compliance with the specifications of any number of producers, network executives, and advertisers, they were no match for even the mildest trolls on a political blog. But the very fact that the show made it on the air at all suggests that the cultural appetite for this kind of confrontation is growing more ravenous by the day. (This past Halloween, a middle-school-aged trick-or-treater showed up at my door wearing a costume that said "hater lover"; later, I spotted another kid in dress proclaiming himself to be an actual "hater"; I hope they found each other.) It makes me think I wasn't so crazy when I once (only half-jokingly) suggested to a colleague that the opinion columnists at our paper should host a "haters picnic," wherein we would cheerily serve up hot dogs and potato salad and give our angriest readers the chance to tell us in person what they thought of us.

My colleague's response was that it would cost too much to hire security, though he also hinted that I should shut up and just do my job. He had a point. Part of our line of work involves being able to ignore the agitators, or at least brush them off. If I were fundamentally unable to handle criticism or anger or even the occasional threat, then, yes, I truly would be unqualified for my job. But there is a world of difference between the traditional notion of public participation in a newspaper or magazine and the cacophonous, sometimes libelous free-for-all that passes for it today. Whereas the old-fashioned letter to the editor involved crafting a letter, figuring out where to send it, springing for a stamp, and knowing that its publication-worthiness would be determined by an actual editor who might even call and suggest some actual edits, today's readers are invited to "join the conversation" as if the work of professional reporters and columnists carries no more authority than small-talk at a cocktail party. And although some sites are making efforts to weed out the trolls by disabling anonymous posting, filtering comments through Facebook, or letting readers essentially monitor themselves by flagging or promoting comments at their own discretion, most are so desperate to catch eyeballs wherever and however possible that they're loathe to turn down any form of free content.

This is by now an old gripe in journalism circles, many members of which will point out that the last word on the matter could well have been said years ago when the *Onion* published its fake news story "Local Idiot to Post Comment on Internet." But if six years ago the phenomenon felt like a wave that was about to crest and then surely dissipate into a vague memory of some fleeting, anarchic period in the history of the internet ("Remember back in 2008 when only idiots posted comments?" we imagined ourselves chortling one day), it feels today like the disease-ridden aftermath of a flood. Ugly commentary doesn't just litter the internet, it infects it. It takes the act of reading an article or watching a video or listening to a podcast and turns it from a receptive experience into a reactive one. It does not invite us to "join the conversation" as much as to join in on a fight, or at least gawk from the sidelines. Perhaps worst of all, it gives the impression that the opinions expressed in those fights are not just the ravings of a few local idiots but the "voice of the people." Spend enough time in the company of that voice and the world will begin to look like a very bleak place indeed.

When I think of the coiners of the term *haterade,* those young, mean/smart, media-obsessed bloggers on mean/smart, media-obsessed websites who seem to be able to whip up five hundred words of clever commentary in the time it takes people my age to think of an opening sentence, I wonder if their brains are wired in such a way that the slings and arrows of free-flowing obloquy don't inflict quite as much pain on them as they might on their elders. The fact that they've developed several playful iterations of the word *hate*—you can *hate on* someone, show some *hatitude,* or simply be a *hater*—suggests that they've found a way to laugh at and therefore defang (reappropriate?) the whole gestalt. But I also wonder how often they get to experience the thrill of clueless abandon. I wonder if they've ever really been able to express anything—in print, on a blog, on Facebook, wherever—without on some level bracing themselves for mockery or scorn or troll-driven pestilence. I wonder if they could write something as controversial as "Safe-Sex Lies" (even in a more coherent form) and expect anything less than a full-blown assault from an electronic lynch mob and a lifetime of damning search-engine results.

Still, for all the ways in which haterade feels like a scourge of very recent vintage, it's crucial to remember that in some aspects the acrimony has always been thus. The earliest newspapers in America were penned almost entirely by pseudonymous writers, many of them up to just as much mischief as today's anonymous bloggers. Benjamin Franklin created several false identities under several different pen names, including a middle-aged widow named Silence Dogood, a gossip named The Busybody, and, his best-known, Richard Saunders, whose aphorisms and predictions became the basis of *Poor Richard's Almanac,* an annual publication, launched in 1732, whose mocking tone went so far as to report deaths that hadn't occurred.

During the federalist era, political opponents Alexander Hamilton and Thomas Jefferson, and their respective acolytes, were hating on each other and on the Adams administration so vituperatively that the president signed the Sedition Act of 1798, a statute that made it illegal to publish "false, scandalous, and malicious writing" against the government or its officials. Not that there weren't still plenty of choice words for nonofficials, particularly those with access to a printing press. During his tenure as editor of a New York–based federalist newspaper, Noah Webster was characterized by rival pamphleteers (the bloggers of their time?) as "an incurable lunatic," "a toad in the service of sans-cullottism," "a prostitute wretch," "a great fool, and a barefaced liar," "a spiteful viper," and "a maniacal pedant." (It's fitting that these barbs made such baroque use of vocabulary; Webster was the founder of the first modern dictionary.)

In other words, angry people of the millennium, haterade in public discourse didn't spring fully formed from the digital cabbage patch; it's part of the DNA of opinion itself. Betty Winfield, Curators' Professor at the University of Missouri School of Journalism and a specialist in mass-media history, sees it as little more than the latest form of public expression. "If you have a democracy and people have viewpoints, this is another way to express it," Winfield told me. "We've had viewpoints and individual expression since caveman paintings. The question is whether you own it." The whole notion of accountability in journalism, she said, didn't start until the advent of journalism schools, in the early twentieth century, when the concept of "professionalism," with its emphasis on standards, criteria, and established procedures, took root in America.

But a funny thing has happened since the rise of professionalism. The tenets it embraced—that some people are more qualified than others, that training and apprenticeship have value, that not everyone can or should (or needs to) gain admission into the club—have become unfashionable. And that is because haterade is not exclusive to the media world. It's not merely an occupational hazard of being a bigmouth. It affects just about anyone who tries to do anything that is subject to public (which is to say online) discussion. It affects the business owner who's at the mercy of random, nameless Yelp reviewers who might well be his competitors in disguise. It affects the physician for whom the few patients who post reviews on medical-ratings sites are inevitably the disgruntled ones. It affects the educator who can't give a poor grade without risking retribution via the websites *Rate My Teachers* or *Rate My Professors*. It takes the very essence of what it means to be a professional—training, experience, sheer chops—and reduces it to a stage act to be evaluated with an applause-o-meter.

Part of me wants to conclude this essay with a manifesto. I'd like to declare an end to the self-torture. I'd like to call on every writer, musician, comedian, cartoonist, chef, glassblower, nail-salon owner to promise right here and now to stop reading his own bad press and concentrate on doing work that's true to his vision and unencumbered by anticipatory concessions to ankle-biters who probably won't ever be satisfied with anything. I'd like to be able to make my own vow to stop looking over my shoulder and go back to writing like the person I was before I'd ever seen a comment board (even if that means taking a little messiness with the exuberance). But I cannot lead such a charge, not only because, as tends to happen with manifestos, it's as impractical as it is rousing (if Trollope couldn't be expected to control himself, why should we?), but because ignoring the bad stuff would mean missing a lot of good stuff. And when that stuff is good it can be really, really good. When the criticism is valid it can be priceless. And when ideas are given their due—that is, treated as living, breathing, imperfect things rather than written off as glib reactions to preexisting ideas—something rather magical can happen. There can be a second of silence during which we, as readers, think before chiming in. There can be a gasp of recognition that reminds us why we read or write in the first place. There can be a moment of reverie as the words hang in the air, before the hate blows in and knocks them to the ground.

Such things are possible. They are just uncommonly rare these days. Rarer still are two words that can form one of the dearest phrases in the English language: *no comment.*

If You Can't Make It Here

By Novella Carpenter

I rode down the mirrored elevator and I smiled up at my reflection. I had just nailed a job interview. It was 1994. I was twenty-two years old. I had lank blond hair and carried an Army Surplus backpack. I would have liked to be a punk and live in a squat down on B Street, but I wasn't cool enough.

Frank and Doris live in a penthouse apartment in Park Slope. In return for rent, I have signed up to clean their house, do the laundry, and maintain their rooftop garden. In their air-conditioned, white marble kitchen, I had told them a series of lies. That I had lots of housekeeping experience. That I had a degree in English. That I was an organic gardener. In fact, I had recently dropped out of college, had gotten in a bike accident that rendered my left foot lame, and was simply desperate for a place to live.

The next day I moved in. My room was tiny and although it had its own bathroom and bathtub, I found out that Reggie, their hairless cat, would be sleeping in my room. His litterbox stored in my bathtub. Minor things, I muttered.

I soaked in the bathtub with my glasses on that night. The tub was too small, my legs hung over the edge. I wrote a letter, telling my friend Rachel that I could see the Statue of Liberty from the bathtub. Some cat sand pressed into my butt. Liberty, I wrote, trying to sound happy with the city. But.

Doris woke me up at 6 a.m. the next day. She showed me what to do: how to change the cat litter, clean the bathrooms, sweep, dust, and do the dishes. She followed me around the house to make sure I did everything right. *This isn't so bad,* I thought. She introduced me to the rules of the garden. Before I go out, she insisted that I put on a terrycloth sweatsuit. It was 95 degrees out in the garden. I begin sweating. She had a leopard-skin silk robe wrapped around her seventy-five-year-old body. She held out a stick and pointed at a weed, "Pull that one up."

At first I thought she would only follow me around for that first day. It turned out she followed me every day. I became her hands and legs. After she or Frank took a shit, Doris would knock on my door and tell me to come clean the toilet. I was on call twenty-four hours a day. When I would go to my room to use my toilet, Doris would knock on my door, "Novella! Novella! Where are you?" I would pull up my pants without wiping, emerge from the bathroom. "What Doris?" The cat insisted on sleeping in bed with me, licking my face at night until it hurt.

I tried to forgive her because she's old and Frank's got cancer but I grow to hate them. In addition to their penthouse, they have a house on Fire Island. Every weekend we drove out there. Doris goes to the King Kullen grocery store to load up before we take the ferry. She brings a plastic bag with her and steals the store's free samples. Reggie the cat and I wait in the hot car for them. He pants, I sweat. Then Doris and Frank amble out of the store, jump into their brand new Lincoln Town Car and screech out of the parking lot, Doris clutching her booty of crackers, frosted cookies, and oily cheese cubes.

At their estate on Fire Island, I get to look at photos of Doris and Frank while I clean their room. They used to be a hot couple in the '70s. Frank wore leisure suits, and Doris's breasts were perky. Swingers. I find a video entitled, *Creative Lovemaking*. The photo on the front shows some old people doing it. I saw something sad in their old age. I felt strong because I was young.

I am not like Cinderella, surrounded by birdies and making friends with the cockroaches. I eat Doris and Frank's food, go through their drawers, steal clothes, read their mail, fart in their closets, pocket money out of drawers, drink directly out of their orange juice cartons. I let Reggie go upstairs, even though he isn't allowed, because I want him to piss everywhere. Then I kick him down the stairs. I know why I do this, I've read Frantz Fanon. He follows me around the house afterward—he likes me; at least I'm paying attention to him. We limp together through the white rooms.

When we go to Fire Island, Doris and Frank perhaps expected me to mingle with the young beach crowd. I try, but these beach-goers stare at my unshaven armpits and white body (pitifully exposed in a sad, droopy baby-blue bikini) then go back to talking about the TWA flight 800 crash. I am disappointed to hear the flight debris and bodies had stopped washing ashore by the time I arrive.

Frank and Doris insisted that I gave them a key deposit of $100. That left me with $50 to my name. Since I need to buy food, I tell them I will have to find a job. Doris became hysterical—I wouldn't be on call for when they took a shit.

She agreed, in the end, to let me work two days a week and gave me a package of frozen hot dogs and a brown apple.

I started working for a temp agency called Eden but it wasn't paradise. The first time I walked into the office, the little man at the desk peered up at me and laughed out loud. I was the only woman there. *Hey baby, what are you doing here?* A lot of the guys at Eden have recently been released from jail. My only skill was dishwashing. On Tuesdays and Thursdays, I get up at 6 a.m., take the subway to Eden and wait for work. I come home later to do my chores for Doris. I am exhausted but can't sleep. Their apartment makes me itch.

One day, late in the summer, Eden sent me to a restaurant/deli housed in Bloomingdales called Showtime! For some reason, the place had a Hollywood theme. There were caricatures of famous actors on a wall—Cary Grant and Marlene Dietrich. I work in the back, washing dishes for $5 an hour. I was made for this. The dishes are dirty when I put them in the machine and clean when I take them out. And wet. And hot. I have to take my glasses off to work. I meet Horace, Uam, Alex, and Patti. Uam winks at me. Alex sings, "You give love a bad name" every time I walk by.

Uam asks where I'm from. I told him Seattle and he asked what state that was in. He reminded me of people in my hometown, a small logging town on the Olympic Peninsula in Washington. I realize that people can get trapped in New York, just like people in small towns get trapped. They can't imagine living anywhere else; they can't see outside their city limits. I told him he should move away from New York; it is so expensive and shitty. He looked terrified at my suggestion.

When Horace took his break, Uam turned on Mariachi music. He told me I can call him Cookie. While I stacked trays, Uam danced for me. He shook his little butt and stomped his feet. Clapped his hands and looked at me with meaning. His dance, which I took to be a mating dance of a sort, makes no sense to me. I could barely find my way around the city, I didn't know the difference between the local and express subways, I had stopped getting my period, and I couldn't sleep at night. This dance was another beautiful, mysterious thing that I couldn't understand. I realized that Uam belonged in New York and that I didn't.

That night, in an act of defiance, I didn't go home to do my chores. I had read in the paper that the movie Forbidden Planet would be showing for free at Bryant Park. When I arrived, the entire park was packed. I order to get good seats, people had been there waiting for hours, saving places for friends. I could smell their take-out. I had been eating a great deal of peanut butter. In addition to stealing from Doris and Frank, I had started shoplifting food at the grocery store.

I sat down where I could sort of see the screen, a little off to the side. But as the movie started and night fell, people started sitting in front of me. Finally, I could only see a sliver of the screen among all those heads and bodies. I shut my eyes and pretended to be content to just listen.

When I arrived home late that night, Doris met me at the door. She opened her mouth to yell, but I just pushed past her.

That night I had a dream. A dear friend of mine sat with me at the wooden table. After we ate, I complain to him in a slow, shiftless way, about my problems. Before we parted, he said, "You have some shit on your eye," I was not surprised to hear about the shit. I shrugged and walked out into a dark road lined with golden wheat.

The next day I called a friend who lived in Boston and told her I needed a place to stay. She said OK.

Like a cat before an earthquake, Doris sensed that I would be quitting. She didn't follow me around, and holed herself up in her bedroom. I did my chores anyway, cleaned the toilets and emptied garbage cans for the last time.

I packed my belongings and prepared to quit. Doris placed a Do Not Disturb sign on their bedroom door. I knocked anyway. No answer. I called her phone from the phone in my room. She answered and then I hung up. Then I remembered she has a phone that can tell her who called. I felt creepy.

Finally I just went to the door and knocked until Frank answered. He led me to her bed. She was all huddled up and I'll admit it, frightening. I told her I quit and asked for my key deposit back. She turned over in her bed and groaned. I would never get that money back from her. I put the key in Frank's hand, nodded at him. I walked down the cool, dustless marble hallway for the last time.

As I passed the doorman, he said, "Leaving?"

"Hell yeah," I said.

To this he laughs and said that I lasted longer than most. He opened the door for me and I walked out into the night with a sliver of a moon out. An old man and his dog walked by while I waited for the bus. They looked at me sideways. "Running away?" the man observed.

"Yeah," I said, and smiled.

"Good," he said.

I took that as a good sign.

Phil

By Kathryn Ma

The first time I met the defendant, and the last time I saw him at his criminal sentencing hearing, he was pale and frightened, unable to meet my eyes. He was in his early twenties, wearing a thin white T-shirt and dark pants. We weren't in the jailhouse; someone had posted bail. Voiceless, with a look of both misery and alarm, he could have been a boy flushed out from his hiding place, rounded up by roving soldiers. When he finally said a few words to me, I was relieved that he didn't need a translator, which would have been a nuisance, as far as I was concerned.

I was probably wearing one of my big-shouldered power suits; I had one in maroon that I hoped looked convincing, and a tan one with black lapels. I carried a briefcase that smelled so new one could picture the cow it came from. It would have been obvious to anyone with a lick of experience in the world that I was almost as young as he was and improvising like hell, a far cry from seasoned counsel, but he didn't have experience or education or smarts. He didn't ask for another lawyer. He took what he'd been given.

It was a small case for my law firm—contraband, shipping, a single cardboard box—but a check came in to defend him, and a file was opened. We named the case "PHIL," not after the defendant, whose name I've long forgotten, but because he was from the Philippines, and therefore "Philippino." This was before new accepted spellings—words like Filipino and Pilipino—took hold to do their part in scrubbing out colonialism, the naming of things being essential to staking an identity, and choosing a history to declare.

How we named our cases was important. My bosses were rebels after a fashion, who branded their litigators' warfare with fond, irreverent gestures: inventive demands in the courtroom, circus-themed neckties, African lovebirds in a Victorian cage outside the conference room where opponents trying to intimidate our clients were regularly interrupted by a quartet of peevish parrots. Around the office, we practiced naming as an art. No bland labels or string of numbers would do. It had to be short and pithy, and telegraph the essence of the dispute. Clever was good, but it shouldn't offend the client. Sly humor raised a round of applause. Competition was healthy, and respect awarded. A case involving alleged fraud and a fitness center was GIMP. Possible criminal claims against a sanitation company became CLEAN. Hyphenated names for clients with multiple lawsuits against them tracked the wreckage like a lovingly documented family tree.

In this case, the defendant, a Filipino, had put two pistols, a handful of bullets, and a considerable quantity of primers into a cardboard box and tried to ship it home to Manila without bothering to tell the feds. PHIL. A name that could have been the defendant's first name, but wasn't.

I didn't want to think too hard about why my boss had chosen me for the case. He was a compassionate man, and someone I worked hard to please. I hoped he'd assigned me because he thought I could do a good job. It was true that I was the only Asian-American lawyer in the firm, but I accepted the logic of the pairing. Maybe my boss wanted to reassure the client that he didn't stand alone, or to press some secret button that would send a subliminal message to the prosecutor and the judge about how the world is composed of many faces, and tolerance of that fact was fundamental to justice. That's what I told myself, so I didn't have to dwell on the sticky subject of race. My job was to be a great advocate, and *what* I was, I reasoned, was part of what I had to offer, both to the client and to the firm. Besides, what was there to object to, since nothing was ever made explicit? It wasn't the first time that my "diversity" had gotten me an assignment, but there was no profit for me in raising the topic. I was grateful for my job. I was working for the best. All around town, my boss was known and admired. He was tall, unflappable, former navy, a former public defender. People came down to the federal courthouse to watch him make his closing arguments in his white suit. My boss was a man with a name.

Our defense was that the defendant had acted at the direction of others, unaware he was committing a crime, though maybe I've misremembered that; the years have passed, and I'm no longer a practicing lawyer. Almost all of what I'm telling you I'm laboring to recall except for what happened in the last minute in that courtroom, a memory I wish would fade like all the rest.

We couldn't claim mistaken identity, but we were convinced that he wasn't working for himself. This was credible, for there are always hard-minded men who use younger men to take their risks for them. There was some suggestion that he'd been put up to the task by powers loyal to Ferdinand Marcos, whose government was falling, but that part was murky. My job was to address the court at the hearing and try to explain (though not excuse) his actions. There was no trial. The defendant took a plea.

I'm sure I explained to the defendant what to expect at his sentencing hearing. This was standard procedure: to make sure the client understood the statement he was making and what the judge might do. The prosecution was recommending a six-month sentence, the probation report the same. The judge had final say in deciding the sentence, but, in a small case like this, where no harm had come to anyone and the offense was relatively minor, the judge would almost certainly do what the prosecutor and probation officer had asked for. Six months seemed to me too long a jail term for what was more infraction than serious crime, but at least if he got six months, my client would be eligible to earn three days off per month for good behavior, and this young man, so lacking in curiosity or indignation that he barely lifted his head when we spoke, was almost certainly going to behave well. Once in jail, he could reduce his total sentence by eighteen days. Eighteen days. Two and a half weeks. That was a lot less time for anyone, especially for someone as unnerved as he was. With credit given for time already served, he could expect to be locked up a little more than five months, which sounded a lot better to me than six. "When you hear six, think five," I probably told him. The judge would hand down the sentence and tell the defendant when to report for confinement. He would very likely be granted a few more days of freedom to get his affairs in order, though what those affairs could be— he was alone, with no friends or money—I didn't ask.

The morning of the sentencing, my boss came with me to make sure I didn't foul things up. All week, I had stood in my kitchen, rehearsing. The talking would soon be over, and our client's future decided. The judge we'd drawn gave us worry. My boss and I had exchanged a grimace at learning who'd been assigned. He was old and conservative, a Reagan appointee, perhaps not the friendliest to a foreign national defendant, PHIL, or to a Chinese-American woman lawyer, CHINK, who would be a new face in his courtroom. We didn't say these things out loud. We knew to hide such biases of the worst, speculative kind.

The federal courthouse is an ill-lit building of hard surfaces and echoing hallways. Our client met us outside the courtroom, downcast and swaying. We talked with him calmly, trying to buck up his spirits. I felt anger at the hard men who had probably put him up to it, though he'd been stupid and evasive—I couldn't change that. In the courtroom, waiting for the judge to take the bench, my boss exchanged friendly jibes with the prosecutor, probation officer, and deputy, while the defendant and I sat together—the pair of us made small by the high ceiling, dark wood, and jocularity of the (*"Write* it!") white men bantering across the polished tables.

"I've been fishing," the prosecutor said to my boss. He was well groomed and athletic, in fighting trim.

"And now you're fishing for men's souls," my boss said. He could get away with murder.

The prosecutor laughed. "That's good," he said. "You're quick." He didn't look at me. He didn't look at PHIL. He stood when the judge came in and spoke his part casually like a boy whistling his way down the lane, rod and reel on his shoulder. There was a brief recitation of the facts, the plea, the six-month recommendation. Cut and dried. In and out. Nobody interrupted.

I stood to speak. "Your Honor," I began. The judge shifted his bulk forward. He was snowy-haired and square-faced and spoke in a bass rumble. He didn't let me get far before he stopped me. This wasn't a bush-league mistake, he declared.

There were armaments, weaponry, a whole lot of ammunition. What had the defendant been doing with all those primers? What did it matter that it wasn't illegal to buy the stuff, only to ship it? His voice rose, and his glare tightened.

I tried to say something about the defendant's background, to humanize him to the judge. This was my job, permissible and expected. The judge mocked me. He drew attention to the fact that he didn't know me, that he'd never even seen me before. I had no credibility in his court. I had lost it, apparently, asserting the rights of my client. The rights of a PHIL. My boss tried for a navy rescue, standing to draw the court's fire, but the judge ignored him. There were strangers in his realm, a worthier target. The walls around me rose, or else the floor where I stood was sinking because a pit had opened up in the courtroom around the defendant and me.

"Well," the judge said, with a sudden, cheerful lilt. He was Santa Claus in robes, handing out surprises. He turned to the probation officer. "What if I give him 179 days?"

The probation officer blinked. His manner didn't change— he'd been doing his job for years—but his tone grew very careful. "Six months is 180 days," he said. "If you give him 179 days, he can't earn time off for good behavior."

The judge beamed. "179 days," he said. "Remand the

prisoner." The deputy strode over. My client's eyes went wide with confusion. I said a few hurried words to him, and then he was hustled away. The judge disappeared into his chambers, black robe flapping. I went to the women's bathroom and cried in a fury, a rough paper towel smashed against my mouth. When I came out, shaking, my boss drove me back to the office in sympathetic silence. What was there to say, when nothing was made explicit?

The probation officer called my boss to ask him how I was doing. "That was really rough in there today," he said. It was. It was. The years have only made it worse. That shit of a judge I remember. The defendant, PHIL, I can't name.

Should Have Stayed Home: Tortuous Trips

My Trips from Hell

By Janis Cooke Newman

"Mom?" my eighteen-year-old son says from the passenger seat of our rental car. "Have you ever driven drunk?"

I glance over at him, phone perpetually in hand, light brown hair hanging into his gray-colored eyes.

"Well," I begin, insanely about to give him an honest answer; "When I was eighteen, it was legal to drink in New Jersey. So it's possible."

"Oh. My. God." His thumbs work overtime on his phone. "I'm telling Dad."

I turn my attention back to the bug-spattered window of the rental and wonder what my ex-husband, a man I count as one of my closest friends, will make of this information.

"While you're at it," I toss Alex my phone, "why don't you text Grandpa and tell him?"

As we drive through the sun-struck landscape of the Arizona desert—a place so arid, I can feel my contact lenses drying up even inside the air conditioned car—my son lectures me on the dangers of drunk driving. After twenty or so uninterrupted miles, I turn to him.

"You realize we're talking about something that *might* have happened forty years ago," I say. "I think the statute of limitations is up on this one."

Then I pull off the highway into the nearest rest stop.

And though I do not actually have to use the squat adobe restroom on the other side of the blindingly bright parking lot (and the temperature gauge on the rental's dashboard reads 115, making me fear that the moment I step outside my hair will catch on fire), I open the door and get out of the nice cool car. Because I need five—no, ten—minutes away from my son.

Inside the stifling restroom, I cannot for the life of me remember why I thought driving Alex to college—a fourteen-hour journey from San Francisco to Tucson—was a good idea. I might have been operating under the delusion that the trip would give me the opportunity to impart some final wisdom to him. Provide us with a last chance to do some mother-son bonding.

Instead, my usually charming and witty son has used this time to point out every character flaw and personal failing I possess. Leaving me with an unmotherly desire to push him out of the rental's passenger side door, stranding him in this parched and barren landscape.

Unable to remain inside the suffocating women's rest room any longer, I return to the car, where I discover that Alex has changed the wallpaper and most of the settings on my phone.

"You're too close to that truck!" my son screams at me, the second we are back on the road.

"That's why my foot is already *on* the brake," I tell him.

For the next fifty miles Alex keeps up a running commentary on my driving. From the position of my hands on the wheel—"too low"—to the way I turn my head when changing lanes—"too weird"—to the speed at which I'm driving—"too fast *and* too slow"—which considering the fact we've been on cruise control this entire time seems to defy some fundamental law of physics.

As we approach the outskirts of Tucson, the bossy voice of the navigation app on my phone begins to direct us to our downtown hotel—though to be fair, by this point, that voice sounds a lot less bossy than it used to. The route is a series of quick lefts and rights, and I've got the phone propped up in the cup holder so I can glance at the map.

"Stop that!" Alex says, grabbing the phone up and out of my line of sight. "It's dangerous."

We miss a left, and then a right. It takes us an extra half-hour to find our hotel. When we do, I go directly to the bar and down two margaritas in quick succession.

The next day we drop Alex's duffle bags in his new dorm room and head out to buy him a bike to ride around campus. Because I have suggested we try one of the bicycle shops near the university, my son insists we go to Target.

Everyone, apparently, has had this idea. The most adult-looking bicycle left on Target's rack has a piece of cardboard stapled to its spokes that reads, *For riders 5'4" and under.* My son who is 5'10" takes the bike off the rack and begins riding it up and down the toy aisle.

"It's perfect," he calls out as he whizzes by.

His knees splay out to his elbows as he pedals. The only way he would look normal on this bike is if he was wearing a clown suit.

"Maybe you want something a little bigger," I venture.

Continuing to ride up and down the aisle, Alex points out that I know nothing about sizing bicycles, that I have never known anything about sizing bicycles, and that most likely, I am incapable of acquiring this skill. As he informs me of this, his eyes appear in danger of rolling out of his head. The only reason we leave Target without that bike is because I have possession of both the credit card and the car keys.

At the bike shop closest to campus, my son sits on a chair sullenly staring into his phone while I pick out his bike, his helmet, and his lock. It's possible he's sulking about not buying the clown-sized bike. Or it's possible, he is sulking about one of the other very many things of which I have no understanding. Either way, I ramble on in a bright, cheery voice that in no way resembles my own to the middle-aged man who is helping me as if that will somehow prove to him that I am not the mother of the rudest eighteen-year-old on the planet. As my son appears to be glued to both the chair and his phone, the nice bike shop man helps me wrestle Alex's new bicycle into the trunk of the rental.

Because, of course, there is no parking near Alex's dorm, I drop him off with a pile of the things we bought at

Target—clothes rack, hangers, standing lamp.

"I'll go park," I tell him, "and ride back on your bike."

"Thanks so much," he says *in my mind*. "I really appreciate it."

Day three is a visit to Bed, Bath and Beyond—a trial under any circumstances. But truly unbearable when you are lost somewhere among the fitted sheets and someone is explaining to you that you know nothing about plastic storage bins, are totally clueless when it comes to hampers, and seem to be completely hopeless about shower shoes. Three items, by the way, I would have sworn my son possessed zero information about himself—particularly hampers.

Behind a display of microfiber blankets I spot the sign for the ladies' room and once again seek refuge in the one place my son cannot follow me.

This, I think, hiding out in a stall, *is the worst trip I have ever taken.* But I know I am wrong about that. The worst trip I have ever taken was the one my ex-husband and I took exactly seventeen years ago when we traveled to Russia to retrieve Alex from a Moscow orphanage.

We probably never should have left for Moscow in the first place. But we already had twenty-five of the twenty-six Russian signatures we needed on our adoption paperwork and we were eager to hold the little boy we'd first seen in that Moscow orphanage seven months before. The little boy in the blurry Polaroid we'd stuck to our refrigerator with a magnet shaped like St. Basil's Cathedral. A Polaroid I touched every day for luck.

But this was the summer of Russia's first democratic election, and anyone who could have provided that twenty-sixth signature was out of the city, campaigning for Boris Yeltsin. So for nearly a month we stayed in Moscow. First in a western hotel. Then, as our money ran out, in a Soviet-era hotel. And finally, camping out in our translator's apartment, while she vacationed in Spain on what we'd paid her until we'd been forced to give up her services to save money.

Each day we took the metro to Alex's orphanage, which always smelled of boiling cabbage, and stayed as long as Irina—his caretaker—would allow. Irina dressed in a white lab coat and men's ankle socks, and was responsible for twelve children under the age of two. After we gave up our translator, she took to shouting at us in Russian, seeming to believe that if she spoke loudly and slowly enough, we—like the children in her care—would eventually understand her.

Alex was sixteen months old when we arrived in Moscow. He had dark circles under his eyes and the wispy hair of a cancer patient. I could see that the clothes I'd brought for him—clothes Baby Gap claimed were for children twelve to eighteen months old—would be much too big.

Most days, when we arrived at the orphanage, we'd find Alex wandering around the big playpen with the other children. Children who had only each other for company and the radio Irina left tuned to a Russian news station. Children who were eerily quiet, who made no sound, even when they fell. Watching them play was like watching television with the sound on mute.

Every afternoon, we left voicemail messages for Yuri, our Russian adoption coordinator. Yuri never answered his phone. He said he was hiding from the Russian mafia, said they were after his money. Although the way he looked the few mornings we did see him—bleary-eyed and stubble-faced—made us believe it might have been because he was drunk. We'd ask if he'd gotten that twenty-sixth signature yet. If there was someone else we needed to bribe. He'd call back days later to tell us to keep waiting and that we should have stayed home.

One day, the metro line we took to the orphanage was bombed. Another day, a government official had his fingers blown off in a car explosion. "I hope it wasn't his signing hand," my husband said. He did not say it like a joke.

The English language newspapers were full of stories about a rival candidate for president—a man who wanted to stop American adoptions of Russian children. Every day he gained a little more in the polls. A few of the papers predicted he would win.

One night in our hotel room, I tried to convince my husband to kidnap Alex from the orphanage. By that time, Irina was letting us take him into the weedy garden behind the orphanage where we would sit on a rusted-out swing set.

My plan involved a rental car, drugging the baby with cough medicine, then driving to Finland. And I think if the uncertainty had gone on any longer, we would have attempted it. Because by then, it wouldn't have felt like kidnapping, it would have felt like rescuing our own child.

But a couple of days later, close to midnight, Yuri called to tell us we'd gotten the twenty-sixth signature. His words were slurred, making it almost impossible to understand him.

The next morning, when Irina made the sign of the cross over Alex's naked body—the orphanage couldn't afford to give away any clothes—and put him in my arms, I said to myself, *I am never letting him go.*

But now, seventeen years later, I *am* letting him go.

I come out of the Bed, Bath & Beyond ladies' room and go in search of my son. As I wander the aisles of juicers and duvet covers, I see other eighteen-year-olds rolling their eyes at their parents, telling them they know nothing about thread count or bathroom scales. And it dawns on me that this is yet another rite of passage, as natural—if somewhat less endearing—as when your five-year-old clings to your hand on the first day of kindergarten.

My son is near the registers, pushing a shopping cart filled with plastic drawers.

I see him before he sees me, and for a few seconds I hold back, thinking how nearly impossible it seems that the small boy we taught to walk in the weedy garden of the orphanage has grown into this lanky, gray-eyed almost-man, this person who is more capable than he yet understands. And I suppose that if pointing out all the things I do not know will help him to realize this, I'm willing to allow it.

For exactly twenty minutes more.

We load up the rental with Alex's plastic drawers. Then, because I learned on the first day of kindergarten that the best goodbyes are the quickest, I drive close to Alex's dorm and pull into a bus stop.

"You know you're going to miss me," I say.

"I know," my son replies. It sounds like the most sincere thing he's said since we left San Francisco.

We get out of the car, and I pile the plastic drawers into his arms. Then I reach around them to give him a hug.

The grief hits me ten miles outside of Phoenix. It's as sudden and swift as the thunderstorms that sweep across this desert. And it does not feel very different from Alex's first day of kindergarten, when I sat in a coffee shop for an hour, stunned into silence by how watching my five-year-old walk into his brightly painted classroom without me felt like the end of something.

I drive for ten minutes or so, tears spilling down my face—probably the moistest my skin has been in days—until it occurs to me that what I'm grieving is some version of myself, that woman who spent so much of her life being a mother.

I look over at the empty passenger seat where no one is lecturing me about transgressions I might have committed forty years ago, or changing the ringtones on my phone. Then, I wipe my face dry, place my hands wherever I damn well please on the steering wheel, and head home to California.

My Bookstore Visit from Hell
(fiction)

By James Patterson

When I arrive, there is a sign on the front door that says, "Come See Our New Toys & Electronics Section!" I pause with my hand on the doorknob. They have a toy and electronics section now? I know how small this store is and cannot imagine where they managed to put it.

As I open the door, my question is answered. Before me, right where the colorful, playful children's book section used to be, are brilliant white, sharp-edged display tables and spinner racks. The bright green carpet I remember is gone. The intricately designed floor displays are gone, too. The story-crammed bookshelves are gone. Everything I'm used to seeing is gone. Instead there are phones, tablets, movie action figures, tech company corporate logos. I look to my left and see a large, plush, angry-looking bird staring back at me.

Dazed, I head over to the front desk where a young woman is furiously scrolling through her iPhone.

"Excuse me, but what is happening here?" I ask. "Are you redoing the kids' book section somewhere else in the store? Perhaps you've developed a second floor?"

"No, sir, we're not redoing it. We did *away* with it." She does not look up.

"But . . . why?"

"They stopped wanting books."

"Who stopped wanting books?"

"The kids. They stopped wanting books." Finally she looks up. Her eyes are glassy. I am visited by the memory of a Philip K. Dick short story.

"We did try to preserve the category. We moved the kids' section to the front, we bought a new carpet, we had contests, author events, signed books, et cetera. But they simply weren't moving. Fewer and fewer kids were coming into the store. And fewer and fewer parents were buying books for their kids. It's a dying area."

"But," I say, still trying to get my head around the situation, "why?"

"Because nobody wants to buy things they don't want to have."

"But," I say (it seems to be my new favorite word), "I don't understand. You still call yourself a bookstore. Aren't you worried that if the kids of today don't read, there will be no bookstores tomorrow?"

"Today we are still a bookstore because *some* grown-ups still read. But we can't change reality. Kids these days simply prefer screens." Her phone buzzes and she looks down again. "You can't force people to do things they don't want to do."

"Why force?" I ask. "Why not just… get them good books? We all know a good book is better than the best movie or game or—"

She cuts me off. "Are you serious? Black ink on *paper* versus millions of pixels on a glowing screen?"

I cannot believe my ears. A bookseller is telling me kids no longer read. Horrified by the twilight zone I have stumbled into, I turn around without saying goodbye—not like she'd have noticed anyhow, her attention again fully absorbed by her iPhone—and head outside for some fresh air.

I sit on a bench outside the store, wishing I had a glass of water, and staring dazedly ahead of me. An SUV pulls into the spot to my right and a woman emerges with her young son. His head is down, of course. He's tapping away at a phone. I see the woman pat her pocket and then pause.

"Oh, shoot, I left my phone in the car. Billy, wait right here." She turns around, leaving the kid beside me. I know kids aren't supposed to talk to strangers, but the author in me can't resist.

"Hey, kiddo," I ask, "what do you think of books?"

The kid glares at me.

"You know," I go on, "do you like to read?"

He squints and looks almost thoughtful for a moment. Then he asks, "Do you know this place's Wi-Fi password?"

"Try H-E-L-L," I say.

My Lesson from Hell

By Lavinia Spalding

"What's going on?" Dan asked, smiling. He nodded at my feet, which tapped to an inaudible beat. My hands were in constant motion, too—fidgeting with my phone, flipping through the in-flight magazine, rustling in my purse, playing with the barf bag. I was like a four-year-old. But I'd rarely been so impatient to arrive somewhere.

We were en route to Arizona to attend a weekend Buddhist retreat. Dan's experience of Arizona was so far limited to a Grand Canyon family vacation and a generic Phoenix strip mall where he once bought albums during a layover, and I was excited to show him *my* Arizona: the sweet, picturesque mountain town of Flagstaff, where I lived from ages ten to eighteen. We'd stay with my oldest friend from high school, Kim, and in the mornings walk to one of my favorite downtown cafés. During the day we'd attend the dharma teachings, and in the evenings drink cocktails at the bar where I was served my first alcoholic drink at age eleven. (My babysitter jokingly ordered me a Coke with peppermint schnapps, and though the owner shook his head and muttered about losing his liquor license, no one took it away.) Above the bar hung framed black-and-white photos of notable musicians who had performed there over the years, and I wanted Dan to see the picture of my father holding his lute.

I'd show him my schools, my jobs, my haunts, and the old stone house where my parents lived for twelve years till my dad was diagnosed with emphysema and advised to move away to a lower elevation. Though I never lived in the house myself, it was the closest I had to a family home. After dating Dan for just over a year—and keeping him at arm's length most of that time—I felt ready, finally, to invite him deeper into my life. Flagstaff was a crucial element. The forecasts predicted snow—they generally did—but my good-natured boyfriend wouldn't mind; it would be pretty, and I knew he'd be charmed by Route 66, the snowcapped peaks, the old train station dusted white, the red-bricked historic downtown square, and all the locals wearing colorful pom-pommed felt hats, walking dogs, and riding funky bicycles.

But I was even more excited for the retreat, and the opportunity to introduce Dan to my teacher, Khentrul Lodrö Thayé Rinpoche. The abbot of a large monastery in Tibet, Rinpoche was wise and funny, his lessons were clear and accessible, and he did a spot-on John Wayne impersonation. Eight years earlier, Rinpoche had singlehandedly turned me into a practicing Buddhist after I heard him give just one public talk, and I secretly hoped he'd do the same for my boyfriend, who was loosely Protestant. I fantasized that after returning from Flagstaff, Dan and I would meditate together.

But it wasn't just excitement making me squirm. I was nervous, too. What if Dan didn't enjoy the teachings? Or embarrassed me by asking overly academic and esoteric questions? What if my favorite Flagstaff restaurants paled in comparison to the San Francisco eateries we frequented? What if we ran into one (OK, five) of my ex-boyfriends? What if he *wasn't* charmed?

I needn't have worried, because none of that happened. Instead, I got sick. Immediately, horribly sick. The teachings began Saturday morning, and at 3 a.m. on Friday, I woke up coughing. By the following morning I was miserable. *Just a little karma working itself out*, I told myself in the shower, hoping the steam and optimism would clear my sinuses. *Just an obstacle I need to overcome.*

The retreat was being held in a conference room at a hotel called Little America, and as we walked through the lobby that morning, past the gift shop filled with Navajo rugs, Stetson hats, and turquoise pendants, I thought of other times I'd been there. The high school prom in 1985—my date a short, ugly wrestler who stranded me without a ride home so he could have sex with another girl. My ten-year high school reunion, where I won an award for having traveled the farthest and got hit on by guys (cute and popular once, squishy and bald now) who ignored me in high school. The night I drank gin and tonics in the lounge with a man I loved who didn't love me but enjoyed stringing me along; he sketched me on a bar napkin and I kept it tucked in a journal, long after he married someone else. And finally, eight years ago, when I visited a relative who was in town for my father's funeral. All that, and the lobby never changed. It both comforted and disturbed me.

The room where the dharma teachings were being held buzzed with friends and acquaintances—practitioners I'd met over the years, family friends I hadn't talked to in twenty-five

years, teens I'd last seen when they were three feet tall. My
sister was there, my therapist, even the publisher of my first
book. I smiled, waved, received their hugs limply, and collapsed
onto a folding chair in the back of the room. I usually claimed
a spot up front, cross-legged on a floor cushion, but Dan's
back was hurting, and after keeping him awake all night with
my coughing, I owed him some comfort.

Rinpoche, perched on a throne-like chair, looked around
the room and beamed at his students. When his eyes landed
on me, he wrinkled his face in concern, frowned, and lifted
his eyebrows as if to say: *Are you OK? You don't look so hot.*
I shrugged, nodded, and smiled reassuringly—swallowing
an impending coughing fit. And when he began to teach, I
leaned forward, copying his words into a small red notebook.

Our thoughts motivate our experience, I wrote. *Because we
have too many thoughts, our mind is not at peace, and we have
inner suffering and turmoil. One purpose of meditation is that
it pacifies the thoughts, and the primary purpose of meditation
is that our mind becomes useable. When we begin to cultivate a
calmer mind, it also affects our physical health.*

It was good information for my ever-restless mind, my
rarely pacified thoughts. But it was looking a bit late for my
physical health. I was a mess—and getting messier by the

minute. While everyone else sat silently, I sniffled, hacked, sneezed, blew my nose, ran out of tissue, swallowed my own snot, and finally began excusing myself every ten minutes to visit the restroom. Other *sangha* members—sitting perfectly straight-spined on floor cushions, red shawls draped elegantly over their shoulders as they fingered their mala beads and looked irritatingly healthy—glanced over occasionally and smiled in sympathy. I smiled back, comforted by the knowledge that they were Buddhists who weren't supposed to feel annoyed by my turmoil and suffering. At noon the session ended, and Rinpoche suggested we all meditate together for ten minutes. I hoped Dan would be able to meditate and that it would change his life, as it had changed mine. Meanwhile I meditated on: *Why this weekend? I feel like a bag of wet donuts. How am I supposed to focus on my breath when I can't even breathe? This sucks. My throat hurts.*

We broke for two hours. For months I'd envisioned spending our lunch breaks holding hands at cozy window tables in my favorite downtown restaurants, dining on delicious organic soups and sandwiches and sipping tea while discussing Buddhism. Instead we roamed the aisles of Long's Drugstore stockpiling medicine, then warmed up canned chicken noodle soup in Kim's microwave and napped in her twin-sized guest bed for twenty minutes. We sped back to Little America, arriving just as the afternoon session started.

Thirty minutes in, Dan started clearing his throat. "Uh-oh," he whispered.

That night, instead of being treated to the sushi dinner we'd promised her, Kim tiptoed around us as we lay slumped on her sofa, watching TV and blowing our noses loudly, juicily. She delivered hot tea and blankets, and we depleted her ibuprofen and tissue. We also spilled Robitussin on her beautiful white sheets, kept her awake all night with our coughing, broke one of her lamps, and (we later found out) gave her our flu.

On Sunday morning, on day two of the teachings, we woke to discover a blizzard had buried the town. There was a foot of snow now, the windows were caked with ice, and it was 18 degrees out. Dan had chills and ached all over, while I burned up with fever. We hadn't slept a solid hour during the night.

"Should we try to go?" I asked, coughing. "We should try to go."

Dan lifted his head an inch from the pillow, and with bloodshot eyes and an anguished look, shook his head once and fell back asleep. We'd skip the morning teachings, I decided, but attend the second session, if only to say goodbye to Rinpoche.

The mind chases after desire, Rinpoche said that afternoon. *The mind wants, wants, wants. We are always under the power of the "wanting" part of the mind. But this desire does not lead to contentment. The getting isn't the solution. It's like salty water— the more we drink, the thirstier we become.*

I'm dying, I wrote in the margin of my notebook.

For the first time at a dharma event, because of my weakness and inability to concentrate on anything beyond self-pity, I felt I wasn't gaining anything from the lessons. When the afternoon session concluded, Rinpoche took both my hands, looked seriously into my eyes, and entreated me to please go home and rest and take care of myself. We followed his instructions, stumbling into Kim's house at 6 p.m. We nosedived into bed and remained there till morning.

Our flight on Monday didn't depart till 9 p.m., and wretched as we both felt, I couldn't let go. I was determined to inflict the full nostalgia tour on my boyfriend before we drove to Phoenix to fly home. I couldn't leave without taking him by my childhood homes, my schools, and my first three restaurant jobs (Bunhuggers, Sizzler, and Mandarin Gardens). I needed to show him downtown—or at least the side-by-side storefronts on Leroux Street: Starrlight, the used bookstore my mom started, and The Collection Connection, my dad's antique shop (now a Z-Gallerie). Fifteen years earlier, when my parents owned the two businesses, they spent countless hours leaning against their respective doorways chatting between customers, and I still couldn't drive down Leroux Street without seeing them there. Even though—or maybe because—Dan had never been able to meet my father, it felt important that he see those doorways, imagine that tableau.

Instead, he napped all day, and I fell asleep under a thick blanket watching *Eat, Pray, Love*. At four in the afternoon, we packed, hugged Kim goodbye (and thank-you and sorry), dragged our bags through the thick snow to the rental car, and scraped ice off the windows.

"We still have time," Dan said as we huddled in the car, trying to warm our frozen hands by the dash.

"Forget it," I whined. "The trip is ruined. I don't care anymore."

"No, let's do it," he said, his voice thin and his face the color of dead grass. "I want to see your world."

I relented, waving him weakly in the direction of the low-rent neighborhood where I grew up. But after a drive-by of three unremarkable houses, followed by my equally unimpressive elementary school, junior high, and high school, Dan's brave front gave way to fever, and we headed south on I-16, away from my quaint mountain town and all its memories. Back to Phoenix and the airport then home to San Francisco, where our doctors called it "a touch of pneumonia" and prescribed antibiotics. We got better, and later Dan described the weekend as a fever dream. But I didn't get my wish—he hadn't become a Buddhist, didn't start meditating with me. His stance on the dharma remained the same: he was respectful and curious and loosely Protestant.

And I was deflated. I'd packed months' worth of expectations into one weekend. Of course, as a Buddhist trying to practice non-attachment, I should have known better. I should have considered the intrinsic nature of impermanence. And as a world traveler, I should have known better. I should have remembered that expectations make lousy copilots, and that every trip is a crash course in accepting impermanence and practicing non-attachment.

Nothing catastrophic happened that weekend. I didn't lose my home, my heart, my family. I lost only the concept of a perfect weekend I'd choreographed in my head, an imaginary experience to which I'd become irrationally attached. But somehow the loss felt more significant. Until a few weeks later, when I stumbled upon a quote from the Buddha— "You only lose what you cling to"—and realized I'd also gained something significant that weekend: the dharma lesson I'd supposedly gone for in the first place.

I Can't Stop

By Bonnie Tsui

Girl in flight, late-afternoon golden light. That's me, biking down Flatbush Avenue in Brooklyn. A warm, perfect September Sunday in the park with friends. Pumping pedals back to Manhattan via the bridge. Traffic is light. Suddenly, a brown sedan which is coming the other way cuts left, against the signs.

I can't stop.

Once I accept this fact, the moment lasts forever, like a thread I can unspool and examine at my leisure. I pinch the brakes with my hands—time expands here, nonsensically: *one Mississippi, two Mississippi*—but the effect on my velocity is negligible. The car keeps coming. I'm destined for a meeting with its right headlight or perhaps the bumper to the side of it. I don't remember the moment of impact—there's a frame or two missing here from the memory reel—but I do remember hearing the sharp crack of my helmet as it bangs against the hood of the car.

When I snap to, life is whirring at its customary speed but I'm sitting in the middle of the street, and cars keep coming. All at once, traffic is cacophonous. My knee throbs. People emerge from every direction to ferry me to the sidewalk. An ambulance squeals to the scene.

I finally find it in myself to show outrage to the skinny, dark-haired driver. "Are you kidding me?" I cry. "You made an illegal left right into me!" I think I am actually pretty upset. But because I generally avoid conflict, showing this feels a bit like I'm playing a part. His mother arrives. She's tearful, apologetic, and afraid I'll sue.

The young driver is terrified. He looks twelve, though his license says he's twenty-one. "I'm so sorry," he says over and over. We exchange contact information, insurance. I can hobble well enough, so I decline to get into the ambulance. But my beloved compact-framed Giant, front wheel askew, won't spin. I take a seat on the curb. The ambulance departs without me; the passersby evaporate. Two of my friends arrive, panic in their eyes.

I'm two weeks away from moving to California, and I've already packed up and ended the lease on my Lower East Side apartment. Back at my friend's place uptown, where I'm crashing, I ice my knee and look out the window at the surrounding high-rises. *I'm fine*, I think. *I'm lucky.* Somewhere inside, there's an unfamiliar little bloom of fear.

At the time, I think I've emerged unscathed. But when I look back, I understand that the day marks a departure from youthful inconsequence. In life, we're a hair away from death. It doesn't sink in for a while. My boyfriend and I drive my brother's dark-green Toyota across the country, our two bikes strapped to the rear bumper. My ride is bionic now, all mismatched colors and tubes; the driver's insurance paid for the repair. We stop in Pennsylvania, Chicago, the Badlands, the Grand Tetons. When we cross the state line into California, I'm excited for the adventure.

But once we get to Berkeley, I'm hesitant about a lot of things, and riding my bike is one of them. Friends who are ardent cyclists say there's great biking in the hills: over Grizzly Peak, on the fire trails around Tilden Park. One afternoon, I skid over some loose sand while taking a hairpin turn on Grizzly Peak Drive. I stop riding, and start walking everywhere. I tell myself it's more convenient, so I don't have to find a place to lock up my wheels all the time.

In New York, I loved zipping up Sixth Avenue with the bike messengers on my way to work. There'd be time for chatting at the lights, and then I'd wheel into the lobby of my building and take the freight elevator up to my office. When we move from Berkeley to San Francisco, I decide to revisit bike commuting. For a few weeks, I pedal to and from home, my new office, and the pool. One day, I almost get hit by a truck. I start driving.

Years pass from the accident, but I just can't shake the uncomfortable specter of mortality from my bike. Then it comes time to take my three-year-old son to preschool. My husband buys a pair of bicycles with extra seats, so we can whisk our two young boys around town. The first time I load Felix on the front, I'm wobbly. Like I'm learning to ride again. His weight throws us forward, grounding the handlebars, which are slower to respond. I'm afraid, but I keep pedaling. My son laughs his silver-bell laugh.

And then we're flying.

Puberty (and Other Pits of Despair)

Camp Showers

By Rachel Levin

This must've been what it felt like, I thought, as I trailed behind the others, buck naked beneath my terry cloth robe, to a cinderblock building the size of a garden shed. Surrounded by overgrown weeds, it was dank and dark, reeked of mildew and hidden away. At night, it was where our counselors went to sneak smokes and swigs, and privacy, a refuge from the rigors of a hot, summer's day surrounded by kids. By day, it was a most public place. We crowded in, two or three, to a rusted metal spout. No curtains. No windows. No tile. No soap. No solitude. Standing under the lukewarm spray, my paranoia set in: *They* were told they were going to shower, too.

At eight-going-on-nine, I wasn't yet sold on the notion of sleep-away camp—a pseudo religious tradition for East Coast Jewish families that requires shipping your kids off to murky lakefronts in New Hampshire or Maine or the Berkshires for an entire month. Typically two.

That summer, I was obsessed with young adult books set during WWII. I read *Starring Sally J. Friedman as Herself* and *The Diary of a Young Girl* over and over. In a sort of upper-middle-class-1980s suburban way, I recall feeling like my German Jewish heroine, Anne Frank, when my parents broke the news that I would be going away to some camp. I had no choice in the matter. I was told I was leaving and to pack my things in a deep, black trunk with brass buckles that I referred to as 'the coffin.'

On the inside lid, my mother scotch taped an itemized packing list, with the hope that all we crammed in actually came back. As we sat on my pink bedroom carpet, folding more clothes than Anne Frank could've ever imagined— Benetton Rugbys and puffy socks and waxy Umbro shorts— we checked everything off: fourteen pairs of underwear. Twelve T-shirts. Five bathing suits. Two sets of towels. One shower caddy.

The shower caddy was another concept I was unclear on.

In my bathing experience, the shampoo and conditioner and bar of Ivory soap lived on the slippery little shelf above the tub, in the pretty white and gray bathroom I shared with no one but my younger sister. Apparently, though, at camp, I was to carry these items to and fro to something called the "shower house."

It would be the downfall of my summer.

My mom and dad drove me north, helped me arrange my yellow Sony Walkman and letter-writing-day stationery on the shelf above my top bunk, and joined me on a brief tour of "Girls' Area." Thirteen creaky log cabins scattered around a balding, dry lawn. All appeared campy and kosher until we took a peek behind Bunk 7: "This must be the shower house," my mom said, stuck her head in, and quickly moved on. She was not terribly comfortable with cinderblock shower houses.

Obviously she hadn't done her due diligence because what Jewish mother in her right mind would want her daughter to be forced to march naked (albeit in a robe and jelly shoes), rain or shine, across the dirt to a cold, damp, windowless cement box that looked like—well, to my eight-year-old-mind anyway—an Auschwitz gas chamber.

"Bye! Have fun!" my parents said with a hug then drove off in their Peugeot, leaving me behind to make Jewish friends, play Newcomb, and never shower again. At least until August.

With two-hundred girls to clean every day, there was a schedule. The oldest girls got the money spot: pre-dinner. I'd sit on the front steps and watch them, the fourteen- and fifteen-year-olds, barely wrapped in their towels as they raced toward the shower house, eager to beat the line, calling dibs on "First hair dryer!"

Being one of the youngest groups, our designated time was after swimming and before lunch. No one else in Upper Alef—aka Girls Bunk 3—seemed bothered by this strange new custom of communal showering. My bunkmates peeled out of their wet suits, donned their robes, and made a mad dash for the gas chamber, plastic baskets brimming with Pantene and Pert Plus. Some girls brought Sun-In, others toothbrushes. ("Brushing in the shower makes your teeth feel cleaner," explained Rasheena Levine, the worldliest member of Girls Bunk 3.)

The eager-to-mature girls unnecessarily lugged menthol-scented cans of Barbasol shaving cream and plastic pink Gillette razors. Rasheena didn't use shaving cream. ("Shaving your legs with shampoo makes them smoother," she declared). And so the eager-to-mature girls switched.

Not me. I had no razor. No training bra. No Frosted Brownie lip-gloss from CVS. No boy I even kind of liked. I might've packed a stick of Powder Fresh Secret under my mom's mandate, but really I wanted nothing to do with such symbols of puberty.

And yet, I was the only girl my age actually, physically, anywhere near it. I would not need a bra or get my period for another four or five years, but, yes, OK: at the dawn of fourth grade, I had … pubic hair. A lot of it.

An unfortunate fact I found, even then, hard to believe. I mean, fine, at my grade school—a preppy, blazer-clad campus filled with smooth-skinned WASPs and Asians— I'd expect it; I was already the only kid with a frizzy head of brown hair. But this was a camp of JAP-y, Ashkenazi Jews—an ethnic group that has arguably kept brow-, bikini-, and back-waxers in business. How, among my people, was I the only almost-nine-year-old in this predicament?

Why me? I'd ask myself like a newly diagnosed cancer patient. Though I'd identified with Anne Frank, I hadn't quite acquired her level of composure or bravery.

I realized, even at the time, that had I been Rasheena, early onset pubic hair would've been a badge of honor, something to parade around the shower house, while offering proper caretaking techniques. But I was not Rasheena. I was a shy, homesick little girl who feared all things adult. The last thing I wanted was to start looking like one.

So instead of showering every day before lunch, I'd cry. My counselors tried their best to help. "*We* have pubic hair!" they'd say in unison, which only made me cry harder. And then one counselor had what she thought was a brilliant idea: "Why don't you shower with the older girls?"

I gave it a go and immediately discovered that showering with teenagers was not the answer. What was every camp boy's wet dream was this almost-nine-year-old girl's nightmare. And being at eye level with the enemy didn't help matters. It was a jungle in there. Boobs bobbing! Nipples the size of dollar pancakes staring at me! Long legs and armpits and bikini lines being shaved. TMI, I know, but the odd tampon string dangling. On one counselor, I think I even saw cellulite. In the shower house that day before dinner, I glimpsed my future. And it wasn't pretty.

After that, I was sent to meet with the head of Girls' Area. She was an older woman who lived and showered as one— unless incarcerated or newly in love—should: alone. She sympathized with me. Or maybe she just smelled me.

Either way, like Miep Gies, she saved me from having to

face a body I wasn't quite ready to inhabit. It was a secret, one I wasn't to tell anyone, but every day for the rest of the summer, she snuck me in. Her tiny, white acrylic plastic can of a shower stall was all mine.

Long Distance

By Chris Colin

My relationship with Cindy McPherson was building
momentum. Not in an old-fashioned and conventional sense,
but rather—what's the word when that lurching rich kid Rat
pops off your would-be girlfriend's bra in a rowboat?

Rumor of the tryst spread through our ranks like the wildfire
I was dutifully on guard against all summer. I was thirteen. I
had a thirteen-year-old's sense of how flames could sweep AT
ANY MINUTE through our piney Adirondack hormone pit.
I had zero sense of how a relationship worked. Or a bra.

Cindy's not her real name and Rat's not his—in reality he
was named for an even more improbable, rat-sized creature.
But everything else here is real, not least my recollection

of Cindy's excellence. She was a brassy seventh grader, one of those always-hoarse girls, shouting and exhilaratingly confident. A spray of freckles covered the bridge of her nose but she was aging out of them, pivoting into a genuine teen. Was she already cutting the necks out of her T-shirts? Yes. Would she have ruled a beach boardwalk situation? Oh yes. Would she have gotten the Led out, like, a full year before other kids in her class? Why would you even ask that.

It'd be impossible to calculate how many long, meaningful conversations Cindy and I conducted that summer. Roughly one. But we had enough superficial ones—over lanyards, by the lake, outside our cabins—to amass meaning. My reserve and redheadedness had branded me a Nice Guy in the dismal camp taxonomy: the kiss of death, or rather of no kisses at all. But I wasn't entirely a lost cause. If she'd started to run with a faster crowd, maybe I offered a welcome break, like a glass of milk after a night of kamikazes.

After camp I returned to nerdy Virginia, and Cindy went back to whatever edgy mid-Atlantic state she inhabited. I sent her a couple letters, she sent me, no, not zero—one. A decent one, too. And, there must've been some kind of follow-up, because somehow that fall it was determined a phone call would occur.

I had phoned friends plenty. I had phoned my parents. I phoned the baseball card shop and my grandmother. I had never phoned a brash, older girl *long-distance* about what may or may not be a future necking arrangement. We scheduled the call and I got sign-off on the long-distance. Regarding the importance of the summer camp romance, I can only say that, to a certain species of quiet, slow-bloomers, a kind of giddy mental hyperventilating will commence at a time like this.

On the night of the call I pushed my dinner around but barely ate. Afterwards, I cleared the table, vaguely cleaned some dishes, and vibrated down to the TV room. At the appointed hour I shooed my family away and dialed.

Cindy's mom answered. A person can get lost in the whole "Is Cindy there" vs "May I speak with Cindy" debate, but I pushed through and soon her daughter and I were connected. She sounded older but it was her. We were doing it; we were talking.

Hi.

Hi.

What's up?

Not mu—

Beep.

Oops, call waiting. One sec.

She clicked over. I took the opportunity to find a more comfortable position on the couch. I remember looking down at the old pattern on the fabric—pale yellow dots on dark green—and seeing it with new eyes. We'd been talking less than a minute but already something had changed in me. I was chatting with a girl from camp. My parents were nowhere in sight. I was a junior high student. The Reagan days were on the wane and soon there'd be another guy, and junior high would become high school, and the planet was circling the sun and I was up and running, I was part of the whole operation.

I noticed on the VCR clock that three minutes had passed. Cindy was a take-care-of-business girl. If she had to deal with a call, she'd deal with the call. I liked that.

The thing about noticing the VCR clock, though, is you can't really stop noticing it. Another couple minutes passed. Was there some crisis on the other line? Maybe, but wouldn't she tell the crisis person to hang on, and click back over to explain? Possibly there was a technical problem, but I couldn't really imagine what it would be. Phones worked pretty nicely back then.

Not a big deal. I had a magazine to flip through while I waited, what did I care? I kept a cool head, and this carried me to the fifteen-minute mark. The fifteen-minute mark is when a person might give serious thought to hanging up, if he hadn't already. I *did* give it thought. My thought was, of course, not to. Hanging up only made sense if Cindy wasn't coming back. But what kind of person wouldn't come back? I mean, who would simply leave a person sitting there with the phone to their ear forever, without even a goodbye?

Did my parents or—worse—my little brother look in with concern at some point? Did I wave them away with oblivious assurance? I'm happy not to remember either way.

Whatever happened, it happened for forty minutes. Then I reached over the end of the couch, returned the receiver to its cradle and went to my room. I don't think I said goodnight to anyone.

How old we get. How curdled and knowing. The TV comes on and we mute it; we know what it's going to say. People come by and we mute them; we know what they're going to say. The Perseids will be overhead tonight, ancient comet dust! *No thanks, saw it last summer.* Our lights don't just blink off at the end. They dim for years.

But for a moment they're bright with a beautiful dumbness. For a sweet, brief time we don't know how the fuck a phone works, or a fellow human. These items are oversized in our young hands, fumbleable. So we cling—to the promise of a conversation resumed, to the hope a heedless redhead will get the message.

Cindy and I never wrote or spoke again. For all I know she's still on the other line. Me, I passed through the standard forty-minutes-on-hold grief cycle: confusion, sadness, shame, forget about it entirely, grow up, find real relationship, ponder how to get my kids to eat tomatoes. It gets better—but in that is a sliver of regret, too. One minute the sweaty phone is to your ear, the next you're a grownup, stable and fat, unhumiliated but also unsurprised by the world. You don't miss phone calls like that, no, but maybe you sort of miss the way they shook you?

The other day, after twenty-six years, it finally crossed my aged mind to look Cindy up. Her name—her real name— is a distinct one, so the odds seemed decent. Turns out two women her age have that same distinct name, according to Facebook, both hailing from the same rough area. I opened two tabs.

Each woman looked like she could be Cindy, and each looked entirely different from the other. The first had a kind and intelligent look; in her profile photo she was sipping tea and looking up at the camera unassumingly. That gentleness was missing from the second. In this picture she was bounding—extreme sports-style—over a pit of mud or something. She had the face of someone who tells you, impatiently, about her CrossFit regimen. She looked kind of mean.

Either could've been Cindy, really. Had that great brashness soured into a joyless athleticism? Or did she mellow into an open and warm tea-sipper? Who knows? But as I went to click out of Facebook, I caught the ambiguous gaze of a third person on my screen.

I've seen my profile picture a thousand times, naturally. But I saw something different on this day. Of course we all see our most uncertain younger selves in photos, no matter how well we've convinced the world we're adults. Now, for a split second, I saw not just my youth but that one evening of my youth. I was camped out on that green couch all over again, ear pressed once more against the TV room phone. Hang up, you cretin, I think. I mean, things work out either way, but hang up.

Orange Crush

By Yiyun Li

During the winter in Beijing, where I grew up, we always had orange and tangerine peels drying on our heater. Oranges were not cheap. My father, who believed that thrift was one of the best virtues, saved the dried peels in a jar; when we had a cough or cold, he would boil them until the water took on a bitter taste and a pale yellow cast, like the color of water drizzling out of a rusty faucet. It was the best cure for colds, he insisted.

I did not know then that I would do the same for my own children, preferring nature's provision over those orange- and pink- and purple-colored medicines. I just felt ashamed, especially when he packed it in my lunch for the annual field trip, where other children brought colorful flavored fruit drinks made with what my father called "chemicals".

The year I turned sixteen, a new product caught my eye. Fruit Treasure, as Tang was named for the Chinese market, instantly won everyone's heart. Imagine real oranges condensed into a fine powder! Equally seductive was the TV commercial, which gave us a glimpse of a life that most families, including mine, could hardly afford. The kitchen was spacious and brightly lit, whereas ours was a small cube—but at least we had one; half the people we knew cooked in the hallways of their apartment buildings, where every family's dinner was on display and their financial states assessed by the number of meals with meat they ate every week. The family on TV was beautiful, all three of them with healthy complexions and toothy, carefree smiles (the young parents I saw on my bus ride to school were those who had to leave at 6 or even earlier in the morning for the two-hour commute, and who had to carry their children, half-asleep and often screaming, with them because the only child care they could afford was that provided by their employers).

The drink itself, steaming hot in an expensive-looking mug that was held between the child's mittened hands, was a vivid orange. The mother talked to the audience as if she were our best friend: "During the cold winter, we need to pay more attention to the health of our family," she said. "That's why I give my husband and my child hot Fruit Treasure for extra warmth and vitamins." The drink's temperature was the only Chinese aspect of the commercial; iced drinks were considered unhealthful and believed to induce stomach disease.

As if the images were not persuasive enough, near the end of the ad an authoritative voice informed us that Tang was the only fruit drink used by NASA for its astronauts—the exact information my father needed to prove his theory that all orange-flavored drinks other than our orange-peel water were made of suspicious chemicals.

Until this point, all commercials were short and boring, with catchy phrases like "Our Product Is Loved by People Around the World" flashing on screen. The Tang ad was a revolution: the lifestyle it represented was a more healthy and richer one. China was beginning to embrace the West and its capitalism, and Western luxury was just starting to become legitimate.

Even though Tang was the most expensive fruit drink available, its sales soared. A simple bottle cost 17 Yuan, a month's worth of lunch money. A boxed set of two became a status hostess gift. Even the sturdy glass containers that the powder came in were coveted. People used them as tea mugs, the orange label still on, a sign that you could afford the modern American drink. Even my mother had an empty Tang bottle with a snug orange nylon net over it, a present from one of her fellow schoolteachers. She carried it from the office to the classroom and back again as if our family had also consumed a full bottle.

The truth was, our family had never tasted Tang. Just think of how many oranges we could buy with the money saved, my father reasoned. His resistance sent me into a long adolescent melancholy. I was ashamed by our lack of style and our life, with its taste of orange-peel water. I could not wait until I grew up and could have my own Tang-filled life.

To add to my agony, our neighbor's son brought over his first girlfriend, for whom he had just bought a bottle of Tang. He was five years older and a college sophomore; we had nothing in common and had not spoken more than ten sentences. But this didn't stop me from having a painful crush on him. The beautiful girlfriend opened the Tang in our flat and insisted that we all try it. When it was my turn to scoop some into a glass of water, the fine orange powder almost choked me to tears. And the taste was not like real oranges but stronger, as if it were made of the essence of all the oranges

I had ever eaten. This would be the love I would seek, a boy unlike my father, a boy who would not blink to buy a bottle of Tang for me. I looked at the beautiful girlfriend and wished to replace her.

My agony and jealousy did not last long, however. Two months later the beautiful girlfriend left the boy for an older and richer man. Soon after, the boy's mother came to visit and was still outraged about the Tang. "What a waste of money on someone who didn't become his wife!" she said.

"That's how it goes with young people," my mother said. "Once he has a wife, he'll have a better brain and won't throw his money away."

"True. He's just like his father. When my husband courted me, he once invited me to an expensive restaurant and ordered two fish for me. After we were married, he wouldn't even allow two fish for the whole family for one meal!"

That was the end of my desire for a Tangy life. I realized that every dream ended with this bland, ordinary existence, where a prince would one day become a man who boiled orange peels for his family. I had not thought about the boy much until I moved to America 10 years later and discovered Tang in a grocery store. It was just how I remembered it—a fine powder in a sturdy bottle--but its glamour had lost its gloss because, alas, it was neither expensive nor trendy. To think that all the dreams of my youth were once contained in this commercial drink! I picked up a bottle and then returned it to the shelf.

Leonard Bush's Leg
(fiction)

By Susan Gregg Gilmore

Leonard Bush wasn't thinking about grown-up things the day he buried his left leg between distant cousins long dead. He was only a boy on that Saturday afternoon in 1982. His skin was pale and his frame slight, but Leonard did not slump or flinch once during the graveside service—not even when a mass of gnats took reckless and determined aim at his bandaged stump.

Words like *destiny*, *calling*, and *divine purpose* swirled about him like the debris kicked up from the tail of a twister. He swatted at those words, too, because Leonard refused to believe that his recent amputation was divine as his mother, born and raised in the Church of God, professed it must be. Leonard could not imagine anyone—on Earth or in Heaven—taking a leg from twelve-year-old boys as part of a grand scheme. Cutting his foot on a shard of glass was the reason he lost his left leg. An accident. That's all there was to it.

Leonard's mother had warned him not to run around the banks of the Little Tennessee with bare feet. "There's broken beer bottles down there, not to mention piles of cow dung, and who knows what else," she'd say while pointing to Leonard's sneakers by the back door. "Put those shoes on, and don't go down there alone. You hear me? Shoes. Not alone."

So when Leonard went fishing with his best friend, Marcus, and stepped on a razor-sharp piece of green bottle glass by the riverbank and his toe spewed blood, he did not tell his mother. Nor did he tell her when his toe turned a shade of cherry that streaked up his foot past his ankle. He did not tell her when his skin burned hot to the touch and his foot swelled up like a tick on a dog's back. But when he spiked a fever and convulsed on the kitchen floor, Mrs. Bush rushed him to the doctor.

A helicopter came and whisked him away to the hospital sixty miles south in Chattanooga. His mother and father followed behind in their Chevrolet Impala. Leonard later learned he had been the talk of Sweetwater for days after that—the boy who flew in a whirlybird to have his leg cut off. A color photograph of him smiling from his hospital bed ran on the front page of the *Sweetwater Herald*. Neighbors carried chicken casseroles and pans of lasagna to the house and stored them in the chest freezer kept in the garage. Leonard's friends left gifts—puzzles, games, coloring books—all things Leonard could do with one leg. *Sitting-down things* as Leonard called them. He didn't care much for games, except for Battleship, and nobody gave him that.

Mrs. Bush cried every day her son was in the hospital, and every day after that for quite some time. She begged the doctor to put him back together, whole, the way he had been when he came into this world, weighing seven pounds and three ounces. Leonard was finally left to wonder if his mother wanted his leg back more than he did. But Mrs. Bush did not want to keep her son's leg for burying as Leonard insisted. She said it was not a prize or a souvenir and that a grave would only be a constant reminder of the worst day of her life. Leonard figured his hobbling around with one leg would be reminder enough.

The doctor explained that the limb would be amputated two inches below the knee. "You'll walk out of here," he promised. "On an artificial leg. Made right here in the USA."

He turned to Mr. and Mrs. Bush and peered at them above the rim of his glasses. "It's even water-resistant," he added.

But when Leonard asked what would happen to his real leg, the doctor pushed his eyeglasses up against his forehead and patted Leonard's arm. "Don't go worrying yourself with all of that, son. Just concentrate on getting better. Moving on with your life."

Leonard caught a whiff of the sick, sweet smell coming from his wound. He knew his leg had to go, and he intended to move on with his life. There was no point in going backwards. But he needed his leg back first. "Something is tugging on me. Can't explain it," he told the doctor. "Seems like it's mine to keep anyway, ain't it?"

Mr. Bush gripped Leonard's shoulder and offered his son a reassuring smile while Mrs. Bush dropped her head in her hands, her red-polished fingernails digging into her scalp. Her shoulders shook, gently at first, but soon harder and more violent till Leonard feared that a thunderstorm might be brewing deep inside his mother's belly. Mrs. Bush pitched forward and fell onto her knees and lay crumpled there on the floor at the doctor's feet, flooding the sterile, white room with her sadness.

Leonard leaned over his bed made of cold stainless steel,

and dropped a Kleenex near his mother's head. Her back rose and fell with each tearful wave while the doctor shuffled a small stack of papers and glanced at his gold-linked watch. Mr. Bush pulled a flattened pack of Salem Lights from his shirt pocket and stepped outside, shaking a cigarette free as the door closed behind him.

Mrs. Bush finally grabbed at the Kleenex, wiped her eyes dry, and asked the doctor if her son needed a psychiatrist.

The doctor confessed he had known other people to request their body parts returned and then again pushed his glasses up against his forehead, something that impressed Leonard very much. "It's usually the Jehovah's Witnesses wanting everything back. They're funny that way. Think they need every little bit they came with to get into heaven at the end. Of course, my own son keeps his tonsils in a jar in the back of his dresser drawer." The doctor laughed and went back to studying his papers.

Mrs. Bush gripped the bed's railing and pulled herself up, knocking into the doctor as she found her balance. "This is not the same thing," she said, her tone now dry and cutting. She straightened her skirt and pointed her index finger inches from the doctor's nose. Leonard looked away, tapping at a balloon tied to his bed.

Two weeks later, when Leonard left the hospital, the leg came home with him, wrapped in plastic and packed in a styrofoam box with ice. Mrs. Bush insisted the leg ride in the trunk of the Chevrolet Impala.

The funeral was set for three o'clock the following Saturday afternoon at the Bush family cemetery, a generous plot of land tucked between two bands of gangly loblolly pines. Mrs. Bush refused to announce the service in the newspaper obituaries as Leonard had wanted her to do. "Really, Leonard, that is just going too far," she said, and snatched the paper from her son's hand and tossed it in the garbage.

Leonard had thought about asking his mother for a new suit, too, one especially made for a one-legged boy, but decided against that. Instead he cut his right pant leg short so his thickly bandaged stump fit clean through without tugging on the fabric. When his mother saw what he had done, she held the scrap of wool to her cheek and cried some more. You'd thought she'd be cried out by now, Leonard figured, but hugged his mama anyway. Then he settled down on the sofa and watched re-runs of *The Rifleman* and rubbed his left thigh, trying to push away the pain that always gathered there at the end of the day.

Mrs. Bush tied an apron around her waist and fled to the kitchen, preparing pounds of pimento cheese and egg salad for the reception at the house that would be held immediately following the graveside service. She whipped up dozens of chocolate chip and shortbread cookies till her skin was perfumed with crisco and butter. She brought Leonard a fresh cookie from every batch and a cold glass of milk. "Drink it all," she said. "You want to grow strong and tall, don't you?"

Leonard drank the milk till his stomach ached, and then he drank some more.

But at night, in the dark, after Leonard had gone to bed, Mrs. Bush complained to her husband. "Everyone in town will be laughing at us, Dillard," she said, her voice seeping through their home's paper-thin walls. "An obituary. A wake. All for a leg. I honestly don't know what Leonard is thinking. His disfiguration has been tragedy enough. Now *this*."

Mr. Bush spoke in a hushed tone, and Leonard could not make out his father's words, even when he pressed his ear flat against his bedroom wall. His mother's voice only grew louder and more shrill in response. "My baby came into this world perfect. He was perfect, Dillard. Perfect. He'll never be a whole man, perfect like he was. Don't you hear what I'm saying?" Leonard fell asleep to the refrain of his mother's lament, but the next morning, Mrs. Bush rose before the sun and made five dozen lemon squares and four dozen fudge brownies.

Leonard and his father arrived at the cemetery early that Saturday afternoon to unlock the gate and set out metal folding chairs that Mr. Bush had borrowed from the church. Mrs. Bush stayed home, setting out cloth napkins and china plates. She doubted she would make it to the service, she told Leonard, there was still too much work left to be done at the house.

Leonard made his way across the cemetery, stopping every couple feet to yank the crutches' rubber tips free from the soft damp earth. His arms were sore and ached from the effort, but for now he preferred his crutches. His stump was too tender, he had told his mother, for wearing the prosthetic. His mother wanted him to wear it anyway. She even promised to buy Leonard that new suit if he'd wear it. "At least wear it to the cemetery," she said. But Leonard had refused.

Mr. Bush, dressed in the dark navy suit he wore to church on Easter Sundays and that now fit too snug across his shoulders, took short, careful steps alongside his son. He carried a folding chair in his right hand and tugged at the red silk tie knotted around his neck with the other. "It's going to be a scorcher today," he said and stopped to pull a handkerchief from his pant's pocket. He wiped his forehead dry and then bent low to buff the toes of his wing-tipped shoes. Leonard appreciated his daddy dressing up for the service. Even his hair, Leonard thought, looked nice and newly polished.

Mr. Bush opened a chair for Leonard and went about pulling dandelions and other weeds crowding his family's headstones. Leonard watched his father work, occasionally pointing out a stray weed or a piece of trash that had blown through the wrought iron fencing that defined the cemetery's perimeter. He offered to help, but his daddy thought it best that Leonard stay seated. "No sense getting what's left of that suit dirty," Mr. Bush said, and pulled at the root of another dandelion.

The Reverend Charles Baxter arrived at half past two, and Mrs. Grissom, the Bush's gray-headed neighbor with a slight curve in her spine, came along with him. The preacher carried his Bible in his left hand, and Mrs. Grissom carried her autoharp in her right, snapped up tight in a worn leather case. Leonard had asked her to play.

Leonard had also invited Marcus and his other school friends, as well as his sixth-grade teacher, Miss Louise

Martin. Miss Martin was the next to appear, and Leonard was not surprised by her early arrival since she always stressed punctuality in the classroom. She hugged Leonard and pointed to her car. "I brought some assignments for you. When you're feeling up to it, of course. And if you need some help with your arithmetic, come to me or ask Azalea Parker. She's such a smart girl, you know, and I'm sure she'd be willing to help you catch up."

Azalea was a full year younger than Leonard but already in the sixth grade. The kids called her "Brillo Pad" and "pencil top," names that mocked her red, curly hair and tall, skinny shape. Leonard just called her Azalea, thinking her name was perfect and beautiful, just like her. He pronounced each syllable slow and soft, letting it sit on his tongue like a savory treat. He sat a little straighter on the folding chair and scanned the landscape for Azalea, but she was not there.

The guests soon arrived one after the other and gathered near Leonard. The women sat on the folding chairs and smiled. The men stood beside their wives and nodded while Leonard's friends fidgeted in place next to their parents. But mostly they all stared at Leonard.

Finally the preacher asked everyone to bow their heads in prayer. He held the Bible over his head as he commanded every man, woman, and child to offer up their sins and shortcomings to the Lord and turn theirs thoughts to God's wounded child, Leonard Bush. As the amens swelled and faded away, Leonard pulled himself up on his crutches, pitched slightly forward, regained his balance, and began to speak about his leg.

He had learned to walk on that leg, he said. He had learned to shoot a basketball on that leg, and he had caught his first fish on that leg. It would be sorely missed, Leonard admitted. "It's been a real good leg." Leonard looked down at the small pine box that sat next to the open grave. Marcus and the other boys leaned in closer, and a clap of thunder rattled along in the distance. "Like I said, it's been a real good leg."

Leonard took his seat.

Reverend Baxter stepped forward again, holding his hands up to the sky. "Please stand." He glanced at Leonard and mouthed, "Not you." The preacher opened his Bible and read a short verse from Psalms. "He shall not delight in the strength of the horse: nor take pleasure in the legs of a man."

The words made no sense to Leonard, but the preacher's voice grew wild as he sputtered on about the legs of men, the strength of horses, and the destiny of God. Leonard swatted at the gnats still hovering about his stump. Finally, Mrs.

Grissom adjusted her autoharp on her lap and plucked the first notes of *Onward Christian Soldier*. Leonard had asked her to play *Let It Be*. But she had furled her upper lip and claimed she didn't know any rock'n roll music.

One final "amen" and it was done.

At the house, men patted Leonard on the back too hard and women hugged him too tightly. All they could offer up were phrases: *You poor, poor boy. Thank goodness you're young. God has a special plan for you.*

Marcus's father boasted that he once owned a three-legged bird dog that ran faster than any of his others on all fours. "You'll get on fine," he told Leonard and stepped onto the back porch with the other men looking for a cold glass of lemonade. Leonard spied his own daddy pouring a shot of Wild Turkey into his.

The boys from school huddled around him on the living room floor and played with Leonard's sitting-down games. But all they really wanted was a closer look at Leonard's stump. "Come on," Marcus said, "Let's see it."

Mrs. Bush, passing through the room with a china platter, said, "No! Absolutely not!"

But when she disappeared inside the kitchen to prepare another bounty of egg salad sandwiches, the boys tightened their circle and Leonard peeled back the elastic bandage, showing off his fleshy, swollen red nub. The boys oohed and aahed at the sight of it, except for Richard Pettway, who threw up in the holly bushes just outside the room's sliding glass door.

By evening, a welcome quiet had fallen over the Bush's home. Leonard was worn out, and his right foot ached even though it wasn't there. He scratched and pawed at the place it should be, but his foot only throbbed harder. He lay on his bed and tried to focus on the shadows jumping across the wall as they did whenever the moon was bright. When he was small, these same shadows terrified him, and he would scream for his father to come and sit beside him till he fell asleep in his father's embrace. Now, Leonard delighted in the shadows' dance. He tried to concentrate on their nimble steps, hoping it would distract him from the pain that wasn't really there. He scooted further beneath the covers and settled into the dark.

As the night wore on, clouds raced in front of the moon but did not fully hide it. The shadows frolicking above his bed only danced faster and harder before finally fading away behind the mounting cloud cover. Leonard stared at the blank wall as he slipped in and out of a dream where he ran barefoot, with two legs, along the muddy riverbank of the

Little Tennessee. His mother was there, too, standing thigh deep in the rushing water, her black funeral dress wet and clinging. She held up his sneakers in one hand and a baby rattle in the other. "Remember, Leonard, how you came into this world. Perfect...whole...perfect...whole."

Leonard woke in the darkness. His mama's words still swirling about his head. *Perfect* and *whole. Perfect* and *whole.* Tears dripped down his cheeks. His shirt was wet and clung to his skin. He sat up straight and yanked at the bedcovers. He gasped and then cried harder. In the dimness, he could plainly see his leg was gone.

Leonard had not thought of himself as a cripple until that moment. Now he imagined his picture on the tin can left on Montgomery's dime store counter, collecting spare change for the Easter Seals Camps outside Mt. Juliet. He saw his friends scattered across an open field, tossing a baseball back and forth, while he sat off to the side and watched. He saw Marcus picking his kickball team at recess, acting as though he didn't notice Leonard standing there in front of him.

For the first time, Leonard realized that he would be the boy who was real good at sitting-down games.

He fell back against the mattress, grabbed his pillow, and held it to his face. He bawled. Long and hard. He struggled to catch his breath but only sobbed some more. He retched, but nothing surfaced other than more tears and wailing. He fell asleep, rubbing at the hurt swelling up in his left thigh.

When he opened his eyes next, a warm yellow colored the room, and the sky outside his window was a rich cerulean blue. Leonard sat on the edge of the bed and palmed his sleepy eyes. His right foot dangled just above the floor while his bandaged stump barely peeked over the mattress. The house was quiet, only the neighbor's beagle one door down could be heard barking at the morning's light. Leonard yawned. Then he stretched, raising his arms above his head.

He saw his leg was gone. But he was not saddened by its disappearance. Perhaps, he thought, God had finally stepped in and helped him along like all the grown-ups had promised He would. Or perhaps burying his leg deep in the ground had done some good. Whatever the reason, it didn't matter to Leonard. He scooted his bottom to the very edge of the mattress. Then he pulled himself up on his crutches and took the day's first step.

Jenny Sugar

By Scott McClanahan

I was in the fourth grade when this little girl in my class got killed.

I showed up at school one Monday morning and Randy Doogan was telling me all about it. "Hey Scott, did you hear about Jenny Sugar? She got killed in a car crash yesterday. Yeah, a tractor trailer hit her mom's car and they're both dead."

Of course, I didn't believe him at first because Randy Doogan was always making stuff up like this. He was always going on about how his dad lived in England, even though this was just something his mother told him because his dad left them and never came back.

But he just kept going on about it. "Yeah my mom saw it on the news last night, and she's dead." Then he giggled and moved on to the next kids sitting at the cafeteria tables. "Hey guys did you hear about Jenny Sugar and her mom? They got killed yesterday!"

I stood and giggled, too, not really knowing if it was true or not.

But it was true all right. We found out just a couple minutes later from our fourth grade teacher, Mrs. Morgan. She stood in front of our class and told us that Jenny and her mother had been visiting Jenny's grandma in Virginia. On the way back home, Jenny's mom was driving behind this tractor-trailer. She was passing it on the right-hand side of the road, but as she was passing the truck pulled over and the car was crushed beneath it. The poor driver kept driving because he didn't know what happened. He drove for another five minutes before he finally realized he was dragging a car beneath him.

So after telling us this, Mrs. Morgan sat down at her desk and put her head in her hands. We were supposed to be working on our spelling words like 'F-R-I-E-N-D-S' and 'M-O-T-H-E-R' but everybody just stopped and watched her. She sat for a second and then she started to cry. It wasn't your typical sad cry. It was a cry a woman would cry if she wasn't our teacher Mrs. Morgan anymore, but a thirty-five-year-old woman named Elaine. I put my pencil down and listened to her cry and thought, Yes. Hallelujah! We're not gonna have to do any work today!

Then another girl named Ammie started crying too.

So Mrs. Morgan walked over and asked her if she needed to go to the bathroom.

Ammie nodded her head yeah.

Mrs. Morgan touched Ammie's shoulder and asked Nicole to go to the bathroom with her.

I leaned over and told my friend Mike, "What's up with that? She didn't even know her that well." But I was just jealous because I wished I could be free, too.

Finally Mrs. Morgan was able to compose herself and told us all, "I know this is a horrible accident but there is going to be a funeral tomorrow and I hope we can all go. I have permission forms you need your parents to sign tonight if you wish to go. I'll also be calling each of your parents tonight."

She said if it was too much for anyone, we could just stay behind and Mrs. Crookshanks would be showing a movie.

Somebody raised their hand and asked, "What movie?"

Mrs. Morgan said she didn't know. She thought maybe a Superman movie.

I didn't say anything but I was thinking—

Superman or the funeral?

Superman or the funeral?

I picked the Superman movie.

The next day at school it seemed like everybody else picked the funeral. Dumb bastards. All dressed up in their nice shirts and ties and church dresses and church shoes. We watched from the window as they got on the school bus and took off.

There were only a couple of us who didn't go that day. There was me, and Debra the retarded girl, and there was Kevin Van Meter, the kid who always pooped his pants. He wanted to go, but since he always pooped his pants the teacher just made up an excuse so he couldn't.

After they all left, we sat down in the dark classroom and Mrs. Crookshanks put *Superman IV* in the VCR. I sat and watched and there was a part of me saying: This is great. This is two days in a row we haven't had to do any work. I mean who'd go off to a dumb funeral when there's Superman playing?"

But after watching a half hour of *Superman IV*, I realized something important.

Superman IV sucked. *Superman IV* really sucked.

I mean you could see the wires that were holding Christopher Reeve up in the air, and the microphone was showing in one shot. Then all of a sudden Debra started crying. I was like, "Debra, shhh, or they're going to turn off the movie." So she finally quit crying. But *Superman IV* wasn't getting any better and to make matters worse I started smelling something.

I sniffed my nose a couple of times and then I turned to Kevin Van Meter and said, "You pooped your pants, didn't you?

Kevin Van Meter kept looking at *Superman IV* and said, "No, I didn't."

"Yes, you did," I said.

"No, I didn't."

"Yes, you did. I can smell it. You crapped your pants like you always do. It's no wonder they wouldn't let you go to the funeral."

Finally Kevin did what he always did. He raised his hand and said in his deep, speech impediment voice, "I'm telling teacher on you."

The teacher came over and Kevin told her, "Teacher, he's picking on me."

But Mrs. Crookshanks smelled him too, and instead of yelling at me, she just turned off the VCR and took Kevin to the bathroom. Shit. We didn't even get to watch the end of the movie.

It wasn't an hour later the school bus pulled back up in front of the school, and they were back. For some reason or other, they didn't look happy. I mean I even tried telling my best friend, Matt Chapman, about how *Superman IV* sucked and how he should be happy he went to the funeral.

"I mean, Matt, it was horrible," I said as he looked away from me. I laughed. "I mean you could actually see the cables holding Superman up in a couple of shots."

But Matt didn't say anything to me.

He just looked at me all disgusted.

I said, "How come you're acting like this and not saying anything?"

Matt shook his head and said, "I just came back from a *funeral*, Scott. I don't care about some stupid movie that my mom can rent for me down at Country Boys. And how come you didn't go? What's wrong with you?"

I said, "What do you mean why didn't I go?" But then he gave me a look I'd never seen on him before. A grown-up look.

For the rest of the day I sat at my desk thinking about how *Superman IV* sucked, and then I started thinking about Jenny Sugar.

I thought about how a couple of weeks earlier my mother took a picture of her at the school carnival and she didn't smile. She didn't smile because she was embarrassed.

She was embarrassed because she'd just started wearing braces. I thought about the last time I saw her. We were both outside, cleaning out our fourth grade lockers, and I was trying to make her laugh by doing a funny voice.

"Hee hee," I laughed in my funny voice, but she didn't laugh. Maybe she didn't hear me, I thought.

So I did it again. "Hee hee."

She just rolled her eyes, shook her head, and went "Ugh" like I was so immature.

But over the next couple of weeks it was like the rest of the kids completely forgot about Jenny Sugar. It was like they were the ones who stayed behind and watched Superman instead of saying goodbye. It was like it never even happened. It wasn't even a week later and they were all laughing again, and doing fart jokes and playing touch football at recess.

I kept asking, "Isn't it strange that Jenny's gone? What was the funeral like? Were people crying?"

They acted like they didn't even know what I was talking about. And then one day doing my spelling words I came across a word. S-K-E-L-E-T-O-N. Skeleton.

I stopped. I looked around, and all the other kids were spelling S-K-E-L-E-T-O-N like there was nothing wrong with it.

I went to the bathroom and passed two teachers in the hallway talking about Jenny's death.

One said, "I think they're holding up pretty well. It's just so horrible what happened." And then the other teacher whispered like she didn't want anyone to hear, "Well you can't even imagine it. I heard the little girl was decapitated and that's why they had a closed coffin. Imagine the father losing his wife and only child in the same day. I know he quit drinking when she was born. I wonder what will happen to him now?"

After that, I couldn't stop thinking about it.

I thought about Jenny Sugar without her head.

I thought about closed caskets.

I thought about Jenny's skeleton and her blood.

Each morning I woke up and my stomach hurt. I was in the bathroom so much my mom started getting worried.

"Are you OK in there, Scott?" she asked through the door.

"Yeah, I'm fine," I said. "My belly's just a little upset."

"You want me to get you some more Pepto?"

I said, "Yes, Ma'am," but I kept thinking about it.

Love and Other Indoor Sports

My Year on Match.com

By Anne Lamott

Heroes come in all circumstances and ages. The prophet tells us, "Your old will have visions; your young will dream dreams." Elderly women in a retirement community in Mill Valley, California protested the war in Iraq on a busy thoroughfare with placards every Friday for years. A man I know of twenty-two, halfway to a medical degree, is pursuing ballet dreams in New York City. Some people my age—extreme middle-age—train for marathons, or paddle down the Amazon, skydive, or adopt. They publish for the first time.

Me? I may have done the most heroic thing of all. I went on Match.com for a year.

The thing was, I had just done something brave, which was

to write a memoir with my son, tour the East Coast together, and appear on stages before hundreds of people at a time. But one dream coming true doesn't mean you give up on other lifelong dreams. You're not dream-greedy to want, say, a cool career and a mate. And having realized this one long-shot dream with my grown child gave me the confidence to try something even harder: to date.

I recoil even from the word "date," let alone the concept of possibly beginning a romantic relationship. Those woods are so spooky. I have an almost perfect life, even though I've been single since my last long-term boyfriend and I broke up four years ago. I really do, insofar as that is possible in this vale of tears—a cherished family, a grandchild, church, career, sobriety, two dogs, daily hikes, naps, perfect friends. But sometimes I am lonely for a partner, a soul mate, a husband.

I had loved the sleeping alone part. I rarely missed sex: I had tiny boundary issues in all those years of drinking, and by my early twenties I had used up my lifelong allotment. I over-served myself. I do love what Wodehouse called the old oompus-boompus when it happens to be in progress, but wouldn't go out of my way. Additionally, I have spent approximately 1,736 hours of this one precious life waiting for the man to finish, and pretending that felt good. And I want a refund.

What I missed was checking in all day with my person, daydreaming about him, and watching TV together at night. There, I've said it: I wanted someone to text all day, and watch TV with.

I am skittish about relationships, as most of the marriages I've seen up close have been ruinous for one or both parties. In four-fifths of them, the men want to have sex way more often than the women do. I would say almost none of the women would care if they ever got laid again, even when they are in good marriages. They do it because the man wants to. They do it because it makes the men like them more, and feel close for a while, but mostly women love it because they get to check it off their to-do lists. It means they get a pass for a week or two, or a month.

It is not on the women's bucket lists. I'm sorry to have to tell you this.

Also, 91 percent of men snore loudly—badly, like very sick bears. I would say that CPAP machines are the greatest advance in marital joy since the vibrator. It transforms an experience similar to sleeping next to a dying silverback gorilla into sleeping next to an aquarium.

And the women are not crazy about the men's secret Internet porn lives. But perhaps we will discuss this at another time.

Yet union with a partner—someone with whom to wake, whom you love, and talk with on and off all day, and sit with at dinner, and watch TV and movies, read together in bed, do hard tasks together, and to be loved by. That sounds really lovely.

I had experienced varying degrees of loneliness since my guy and I split up. After our breakup, I had just assumed there would be a bunch of kind, brilliant, liberal, funny guys my age to choose from. There always had been before. Surely my friends would set me up with their single friends, and besides, I am out in the public a lot doing events at bookstores and political gatherings, the ideal breeding ground for my type of guy. But I hadn't met anyone.

People don't know single guys my age who are looking for single women my age. A sixty-year-old man does not fantasize about a sixty-year-old woman. A seventy-year-old man might. And an eighty-year-old—ooh-la-la.

Almost everyone wonderful that my friends know is in a relationship, or gay, or cuckoo.

I went onto Match.com with a clear knowledge that

relationships are not the answer to lifelong problems. They're hard, after the first trimester. People are damaged and needy and narcissistic. I sure am. Also, most men a single woman meets have been separated or divorced for about twenty minutes.

The man of my most recent long-term relationship, whom I'd been with nearly seven years, was in a new, committed relationship about three weeks after we split up.

I am not kidding. You can ask him. We're very friendly.

So I signed up at Match.com. This subscribing means you can communicate with people at the site, instead of just studying their profiles, questionnaires, preferences and photographs for free. I subscribed and answered the questions.

My preferences are: smart; funny; kind; into nature, God, reading, movies, pets, family, liberal politics, hiking; and I prefer sober, or sober-ish.

So the first morning, eight profiles of men varying in age from fifty-four to sixty-three arrived by email. Most seemed pretty normal, with college degrees, which I don't have, but certainly meant to; some attractive, mostly divorced but some like me, never married, some witty, some dull, sort of like real life.

Curiously, almost without exception, they were "spiritual but not religious." I thought for a while that this meant ecumenical, drawn to Rumi, Thomas Merton, Mary Oliver. But I have come to learn that this means they think of themselves as friendly. They are "glass half-full kind of people." That's very nice. They like to think that they are "closest to Buddhism," and "open to the magic that is all around us." They are "people-people." They are "open-minded and welcome all viewpoints." They are rarely seeking religious nuts like myself—rather, they are seeking open, non-judgmental women. (The frequent reference to wanting a non-judgmental woman makes a girl worry: What if you're pretty non-judgmental, but then Larry Craig asks you out for coffee, or Buzz Bissinger, and little by little, more is revealed?) A strangely high number of them mention that they hope you've left your baggage at the airport—because, I guess, they are all well! I love this so much.

Eight new guys arrived every day, along with a remnants section of men who lived pretty far away. Some of my eight guys were handsome, if you could believe their profiles, and in my case the profiles tended to be pretty legitimate. They mentioned that they drank moderately, or never, or socially (the most you can admit to. There is no way to check for "drinks alcoholically").

For my maiden voyage, I had coffee with an accomplished

local man, who said his last girlfriend had been religious, a devout Jew, and this had driven him crazy. I said I was probably worse. We parted with a hug.

I selected a nice-looking Englishman with grown children for my second date. He said he had a good sense of humor, loved movies. He was, perhaps, the tiniest bit fat. I don't care much about weight, or hair loss. I emailed, and we arranged to meet at a Starbucks halfway between our homes, on a Sunday morning before my church.

This is a true story: He was ten minutes late, and shaken, because he had just seen a fatal motorcycle accident on the Richmond San Rafael Bridge. He had stopped to inspect the body because he was worried that it was his son, although his son rode a dramatically different brand of motorcycle. He had gotten out, talked to the police, and gotten a peek at the corpse. This sort of put the kibosh on things for me. I recommended that we reschedule to a day when he hadn't seen any dead people. He wanted to proceed. I got him a nice cup of tea.

I liked him, though, and we exchanged adorable and kicky emails, arranging another date for sushi, and he was lively, cultured, and sort of charming. But at lunch, he accidentally forgot to ask me anything about my life during the first forty-five minutes of the conversation. It was fascinating, that we did not get around to me until that one question. Then I got cut off.

My pointing this out politely in an email the next day did not sit well.

The next guy was also highly cultured, a creative venture capitalist, who was familiar with my work, and turned out to be a truly excellent conversationalist. We had a coffee date, a long walk on the beach, a candlelit dinner, texts and emails in between, definite chemistry, and then I didn't hear from him for five days.

If I wanted to go for five days without hearing from a man with whom I had chemistry and three almost perfect dates, I would repeat junior high.

My friends were great. They turned on the man immediately. (Of course, I mostly talked to my single friends and to Sam, my son, about Match.) They knew how brave it was of me to go on dates. I was their role model.

This pattern repeated—a flurry of dates, followed by radio silence on the man's part—and made me mourn the old days, when you met someone with whom you shared interests, chemistry, a sense of humor, and you started going out. After a while—OK, who am I kidding, sometimes later that day—you went to bed with him, and then woke up together, maybe shyly, and had a morning date. Then you made plans to get together that night, or the next, or over the weekend.

But that is the old paradigm. Now, if you have a connection with a Match.com man, he might have nice connections with two or three other Match.com women, too, and so each date and new dating level—coffee, a walk, lunch, and then dinner—is like being on a board game, different colored game pieces being moved along the home path in Parcheesi.

Every few weeks, I went out with a new man and practiced my dating skills—i.e., listening, staying open, and bringing the date to a friendly close. My son has "We don't give up" tattooed on his forearm, which is sort of our family crest. So I didn't give up, even when that day's date had an unbuttoned tropical shirt, or explained that there is no real difference between Republicans and Democrats.

Sam told me not to give up, that I would meet a guy who was worthy of me, quote unquote. That made the whole year worthwhile.

One of the bad coffee dates was a kingly little man who bore an unfortunate resemblance to Antonin Scalia, complete with tasseled loafers, who was snotty and disappointed until he figured out that I was a real writer. Then he wanted to be my BFF.

I saw the profile of a handsome religious man, who had graduate degrees, a great sense of humor, and did not look like Antonin Scalia. He said he believed in courtesy and friendliness. OK, I'll bite. The only iffy answer on his questionnaire was that he was "middle of the road."

I dropped him a line.

He wrote back fifteen minutes later. "Your politics are abhorrent to me."

I loved that. "Middle of the road" almost always means conservative, I promise. It means the person is Tea Party but would consent to getting laid by a not-hysterical liberal, which rules me out.

A man with a graduate degree, great sense of humor, spiritual but not religious, wrote to say he loved my work and felt we were kindred souls. We met at Starbucks. He was very sweet and open, but had a compulsive Beavis and Butt-head laugh. After ten minutes of this, my neck went out on me, like one of the Three Stooges.

Then I met a man who was as far to the left as I am, in the weeks before the presidential election! Heaven. He was English also. I am powerless in the face of foreign accents.

Or rather, I used to be.

We went out four times in rapid succession, for coffee, lunches, a hike. We had chemistry, laughed a lot, sent lots of emails. But we didn't touch. I thought, in my mature and/or delusional way, that this would come, but it didn't. I made a few practice casual touches, but he didn't respond.

My consultants said that I should pay attention to this. Part of me didn't believe them—this guy knew we weren't on hikingpals.com. We both wanted mates. But then I got it, that my horrible friends were right, and he didn't feel physical with me. I felt teary and surprised. I wrote to him, with my email voice high in my throat, saying that maybe it wasn't going to happen, and maybe we should take a break while I went out of town.

He said he wanted to pursue this and for me not to throw in the towel.

Hooray. My heart soared like an eagle. We stayed in touch by email while I was gone, for a couple of weeks.

I got home. He asked me out to lunch, and we had an easy, entertaining time. He wrote that he had really enjoyed it. I asked him if he wanted to go for a hike Thanksgiving morning, before the hordes and riff-raff arrived at my house. We had coffee in the kitchen with my son and younger brother,

Neighbors

By Wendy Spero

I clutch my pillow as I'm startled out of an Ambien-induced sleep. My husband Amos, lying next to me, rubs his eyes and groans, "It's OK, babe. She's almost just about done I think." We lie motionless and blink in unison, like two sets of cartoon eyes in pitch blackness, and listen to our 25-year-old neighbor complete yet another absurdly over-the-top orgasm.

As soon as Neal and Karen, a wholesome-looking couple in their early twenties, took the plunge and moved in together—into the apartment below us—they embarked on their we-just-moved-in-together-let's-play-house-we're-so-in-love-ohmigod sexcapades. The accompanying sounds were on the verge of deafening. Neal emitted low grunts and Karen screeched like a rare bird featured on Animal Planet. The images that came to mind were highly disturbing because the couple is a profound physical mismatch. Karen is one of the prettiest girls I have ever seen (long curly black hair, luscious lips, tall) but her boyfriend is, well, not pretty. He's awkwardly skinny and sports a large pulsating canker sore on his lower lip. So while listening to the noises, we couldn't help but feel strongly that these people really shouldn't be having sex in the first place. *It defied science.* Still, my husband and I were initially amused by all of it—in a "yeah, heh, we've been there, those were fun times" kind of way. We were also amused that we were actually experiencing a clichéd joke portrayed in far too many romantic comedy movies or TV shows about couples forced to listen to neighboring couples having far hotter sex than they have.

But after a few weeks, the sounds started to seriously interfere with sleep. And listening to their Beginning Sex really made it harder to enjoy our We've-Been-Together-For-Ten-Years-So-We-Don't-Even-Really-Remember-The-Beginning-Sex. In fact, we were not having much sex at all because I was in the throes of ongoing dental surgeries. My husband and I would listen to hot young Karen cum as I'd lie in bed in my striped, red footie pajamas reading *The Power of Now*—with a heating pad on my stomach (upset from the antibiotics) and an icepack on my face, the novacaine just wearing off. I would turn to Amos, drool a little and slur, "We can do it if you want."

Amos finally admitted that her sounds had turned him on at first, but that the sheer loudness was starting to gross him out. We concurred that she was simply overdoing it. Perhaps trying to get in the zone by forcing more volume or perhaps getting off on being heard. (The latter seemed unlikely, because they were the neighborliest neighbors of all time.) Regardless, after his admission, I started to worry that the sounds were going to convince my husband that I was The Most Unattractive Wife Ever.

I began banging the floor with a broom. But since they used techno music to support their mismatched love-making, they didn't notice. I concluded that Amos had to talk to Neal directly. Man to man. In passing. Sooner rather than later. But he refused.

One night, when our neighbors seemed to have actually taken a well-earned night off, I started listening to a mind-body relaxation hypnotherapy CD, which claims to diminish physical discomfort. It consists of one track, performed by a British man named Michael Mahoney, who is definitely the calmest person in existence. He tells you to imagine yourself pushing a cart filled with parcels up a hill. He tells you the parcels represent your physical pain and asks you to imagine yourself stopping by a wishing well and dropping each parcel into the water. I was in the midst of dropping a large dental pain parcel when Karen's squealing suddenly began. More staccato than usual. "Ah. Ah. Ah. Ah." They were seeping through the floorboards like toxic fumes. I concentrated on Mr. Mahoney's orders: "If you hear sounds during this process, then hear them, and let them go." But I couldn't let them go. I could only imagine myself throwing my parcel on the ground, kicking the well, and anxiously waiting for Karen to finish already so I could continue with the necessary goddamn drop.

I sat up and threw my icepack against the wall. I yanked the heating pad cord out of its socket. I threw the covers off, marched to the other side of the room, and turned off the CD player.

I straddled my husband. "Wake up! WAKE UP!" I yelled.

"Wha? It will quiet soon, babe," Amos mumbled. "Get off of me. I'm sleeping."

I pulled off his pajama bottom scrubs.

"What are you doing? I'm too tired," he whined. "Who are you? Not now. It's 2 a.m.!"

"*NOW.*" I said, angrily. "*Power. Of. Now.*"

Like a mother who lifts a car to save her trapped baby, I dragged my hearty husband off the bed, moved the bed inward so the headboard would bang against the wall, pushed him back on the bed, and savagely unzipped my striped footie pajamas. I ran to the bathroom and splashed my collarbone with suffocating amounts of DKNY Midnight and pulled out every remotely cleavage-y stripper dance move I could fathom to convince my man to step up. We started making out and I imitated every sound Karen had ever made. Amos followed my lead.

What resulted was the most intense sex ever. It was beyond make-up sex, it was beyond honeymoon sex, it was beyond we-just-moved-in-together-let's-play-house-we're-so-in-love-ohmigod sex. It was sex with a *serious* cause. It was get-back-at-your-lame-ass-neighbors sex.

I highly recommend it.

By the time we were done, the sounds below had subsided. It was unclear whether Karen and Neal had gotten the message or had finished their nightly business in a timely fashion. It didn't even matter. Despite exhaustion and dental pain parcels in need of being dropped off, together we did what needed to be done. We out-fucked the twenty-year-olds—if only for one night.

The concept of sex returned to our consciousness. So much so that one night a few weeks later, when we stayed at our friend's amazing pool-house while she was away (she had offered us a mini vacation), Amos suggested we try get-back-at-your-neighbors sex in the hallway by her kitchen.

Please note that get-back-at-your-neighbors sex is not risk free and *may* result in pregnancy. You might want to use a condom if you aren't on the pill, especially if your husband is bad at pulling out. So yes, we conceived a baby, a bit out of spite, in our friend's kitchen area. After praying she'd find it amusing, we eventually had to tell her. At our baby shower, which she threw for us at her house, she created a shrine at the spot where it had all gone down. Yes, it's a tad embarrassing. But I think it beats the whole "we made you on our very special trip to Italy on Valentine's Day" thing.

And a crying baby is the Ultimate Neighbor Revenge.

Hooters is a Restaurant and Putt Putt is for Lovers: My Early Nineties Date from Hell

By Michelle Richmond

In certain parts of the South, Hooters is considered a fine dining experience. It was Alan who took me there and when I look back on my time with him, I always think of beepers.

Alan was the very good-looking maître d' of the Buckhead Club, an establishment I frequented on occasion with a vivacious woman named Dalian, who was, for a time in Atlanta, a kind of benefactor to me. I was in my early twenties, a couple of years out of college, and I had decided that I would be a writer. I'd been living in Knoxville, Tennessee, working for an ad agency, when I found Dalian in a classified ad in *Poets and Writers* magazine, wrote her a letter of application, and ended up in her warm, book-filled house, a "writer-in-residence" before I'd published anything more substantial than catalog copy and letters to the editor.

In addition to offering me a place at her table, Dalian offered me entry to her social set, which was a strange, exciting mix of foreign dignitaries, one-time beauty queens, artists, poets, practitioners of tantric yoga, lonely men in the construction business, and elderly Southerners from good families. Falling into the latter category was a sweet, genteel lady named Clarice, whose fine apartment was stacked floor to ceiling with true "art," the kind that gets donated to museums, and who once read my palm and told me I'd become "successful in business" around the age of forty. Clarice was refined in the way my people weren't. I too am Southern, but my people were sharecroppers and preachers, while hers reeked of gubernatorial grace and wealth going back generations.

Dalian liked to take us to the Buckhead Club, where you could sip champagne and have brunch on fine china with a view out over Atlanta. It was there that I met Alan, who was very tall and had a very deep voice. When he said, "How are you ladies today?" the vibe he gave off was more Captain Picard than Matthew McConaughey. On the day in question, Clarice gave me a not unkind once-over and said of my lavender dress (which wasn't silk but something like it, and which showed no skin but plenty of curves), "That dress is very snug on you, dear."

When Alan came by to inquire about our comfort, Dalian suggested that he take me for a tour of the club. He conceded that there was a room with a particularly grand view that was not in use at the moment, and that I ought to see it. As I was trying to remember where to put my napkin—did it go on the table or on my chair?—Clarice muttered, "Really quite snug, dear."

I don't remember a view, but I do recall a very long mahogany table with a high sheen. As we were heading back out to the land of champagne and teacups and hollandaise, Alan asked me on a date. I said, "Well, now that we've come this far." He was so handsome in his suit that I failed to be alarmed by the fact that he wore a beeper, which is what all men who were cheating on their girlfriends wore before cell phones were ubiquitous. Beepers were a convenient arrangement (some of you might remember), because the girlfriend could reach you but you would not be expected to respond until you could "get to a phone." Already, pay phones were disappearing. The beepers were beeping. It was a time of great sexual freedom helped along by a dying technology.

On the morning of the date, Alan picked me up in a long, black sedan with tinted windows. I hadn't realized that it would be a double date, or that the other fellow would be accompanied by an employee of one of the city's many strip clubs. Our first stop was Putt-Putt Golf. Much ado was made over the angle at which one should hold the putter. It seemed a cheap trick; if he wanted to pull that one, couldn't we have at least played real golf? With the sun beating down on the Astroturf, I realized that Alan looked different out of context, with the brunch patina worn off—out of the suit and into the slacks and white leather sneakers. I despise slacks, especially while playing mini golf.

After putting the pastel balls into the shark's mouth, our double-date friends were hungry. We all climbed into the sedan. Noises emanated from the back seat. I wanted to jump out of the moonroof, but it seemed logistically unsound. After an hour or so in Atlanta's infamous traffic, we pulled up in front of a strip mall. I asked where we were going for lunch. "Hooters," Alan said. "For the wings."

I don't remember the wings. I do remember that there was a television over the bar with some sort of game playing loud enough to drown out Jimmy Buffet. The air conditioning was on way too high, like it always is in the South, and

I thought the servers must be freezing, on account of the orange short-shorts.

The girl who was on the date with Alan's friend asked our server, "How do you tie your shirt like that?" The server unknotted it and proceeded to talk us through the procedure. I drank a lot of beer. Alan's beeper kept going off. It was holstered on his belt in some strange contraption, like a gun, and every time the beeper went off he'd unstrap it from the contraption and glance at the tiny red numbers. If I were from the future I might have told him, "Just wait until we have text messages, with actual words and stuff," but instead I just said, "That might be an emergency. You should call." He said, "Nah, it can wait." I wanted it to be an emergency so that I could tell him to go on home and take care of it. I wanted to be all like, "No, no, don't worry. I'll use that pay phone over there and call somebody to come get me."

If I'd just waited a couple of years to go on a date with Alan, I would have had a flip phone. The mass distribution of the flip phone changed everything. Once the flip phone came around, there was nothing you couldn't get out of. Whenever you found yourself in an uncomfortable situation, you could pretend to take a call from your best friend, who'd just had a terrible rollerblading accident on the way to the tanning salon. With the advent of the flip phone, no woman would ever have to be trapped at Hooters with a man in slacks and white leather sneakers.

My Girlfriend from Hell

By Brian Doyle

Well, the *opening* chapters were fun. The shy glances and the yearning from afar and the first halting conversations like mysterious, alluring chess games. Then the first sort-of-dates but not *really* dates—although of course they *were* dates though neither of us would admit it. The first few doing of things I would never do in a million years except if there was the possibility of a girl at the end. Like hang-gliding. The first weekend away to a ski lodge and not skiing. The first time I met the parents, which turns out to always be fun and terrifying, no matter who the parents are, or the girlfriend is; there's such poignant loss and memory and comedy and curiosity and worry and astonishment in the air, as the dad

154

passes me the meatloaf and stares into my craven soul and does his best to leave a silent message in my heart that if I hurt his daughter he will skin me with a butter knife without the slightest regret or compunction.

But then things went sour in a hurry. I pretended to love her, though I did not love her; that is the nut of the matter, and the real reason she was the girlfriend from hell is because it turns out I was the boyfriend from hell—the charming liar, the personable phony, the eloquent fool, the highly educated dolt, the king of the sin of omission, the boy not brave enough to be a man and stand up straight and tell her bluntly and gently, I do not love you, and you can do much better, and you deserve a man who will love you, and that man is not me, and will never be me.

But I did not tell her that, and was cruel or greedy or selfish enough to let her slowly discover that for herself, which may explain the rage of the closing chapters, which went on for months.

She kicked my car radio to death in a fit of fury. She threatened to kill herself and leave a note that I was responsible. She threatened to have me killed by her violent friends. She said that she would go to the local gang lord and ask for me to be professionally beaten by people who knew their awful craft very well indeed. She screamed in private and in public. We broke up and got back together ten, twenty, thirty times, bitterly and angrily and wearily. My friends laughed at my discomfiture for a while, and then they felt bad for me, and then they grew furious at me for such a tawdry circus, and they were right to be furious. One friend grabbed me by the throat and roared at me for being a fool and a coward, for wasting my life and hers and those of the friends who liked me and were enduring this long, slow, sad car crash with genuine sadness, and he was right, too, although I swung at him then, and realized he was right only later.

Worst girlfriend ever. Three months of real interest and shy pleasure, and then nine months of dismay and fear and pain. Weary beyond words of every argument and fight and shriek and accusation and snarl and sob. In the end we hated each other. What a terrible thing to say. I did not love her, and shouted so many times, and she was so angry that it had taken me so long to finally be honest that she would not let me go. People are complicated in ways we may never finally understand, for all our brilliant analysis and science and art.

Yes, it ended. I moved away. A wise and brave friend rented a house far away on an island for him and me, and he committed to the lease so I could not evade the commitment, and he helped pack my stuff, and we drove up to the island, and I never saw her again. I remember that the phone would ring and ring at that house, and I would never answer it. Not once, in a year, even when I was pretty sure it was friends or family or the landlord. Not once. Isn't it odd how we remember everything, if only we find the right key to unlock the memory we thought was lost forever? I have not thought of that ringing phone for thirty years, but here I am, right now, thirty years ago, sitting in the sunroom of that house by the sea, staring out at the ocean, and the phone in the kitchen is ringing and ringing, in that brassy, rattling, echoing shrill way that phones ring in small, wooden kitchens, and I am staring at the sea, and I will never answer it. Never.

Desperate Times, Desperate Measures

My Year of Heroin and Acne

By Chloe Caldwell

I got a pedicure each time I promised myself I'd stop doing heroin—which is to say, I got pedicures all summer. Pedicures gave me the false notion that I was about to get it together. I wasn't functioning well—my brain cells were spent and my serotonin was depleted. Sitting in a chair, despondent, was all I felt like doing.

My acne had taken over any joy in my life at that point, and I was having opiate withdrawal, so I'd go to the nail salon in the middle of the day when it was quiet and I could avoid seeing other humans. I liked eating the candy from the candy bowl. I took handfuls of Dum Dum pops, peppermints, butterscotch, and those strawberry candies with the gooey middle that grandmothers always have. I sat in the massage chair, crunched on my candies and watched Lifetime movies with subtitles. I pushed buttons on the remote to control the strength of the massage, and I drifted off. I hated myself. I actually hated myself.

I never got manicures. They would be too much work, sitting upright and making small talk. Plus, I bite my fingernails down too low for them to be manicured. A disgusting habit, but in comparison to my other addictions, I let it slide. I have too many battles to fight with myself, so I choose them carefully.

Last June, after one of my pedicures, I left the nail salon and got into the car. I don't say *my* car, because I shared it with my dad. I was living with him at the time, and we shared everything—the bathroom, food; we even worked together at his music store. The car was an eggplant-colored PT Cruiser. I checked my phone. My mom had left me a voicemail, asking me to go on a hike with her before she left for Costa Rica. I would have rather done anything than go on a hike, but I drove to meet her instead of starting a fight. I was wearing flip-flops because it was a spur-of-the-moment hike and I didn't want to ruin my pedicure. As we hiked, I couldn't speak. My jaw was locked. *Oh Mom. Mom. Mom. Mom.*

Help me, I thought in my head. *Help me, Mom. Please help me.*

My mom knew I was depressed, but she didn't know why. We sat on a log when we reached the top of the hill. Sometimes all my mother has to do is touch me the right way and I'll tell her anything. She was doing those things, saying, "What is it, Chloe?" but I knew I couldn't put that burden on her. Tears streamed down my face. She put her arm around me and we sat on the log for a long time. "Wow, did you just get your feet done? They look beautiful," she said. When we parted ways I told myself that was it. No more heroin. I drove away from the woods in my flip-flops, listening to mainstream rap on the radio. The color of the toenail polish I'd chosen was called Cha-Ching Cherry.

To say that my year of heroin and acne was dark would be an understatement. The cycle went like this: The worse my skin got, the more stressed I felt, and the more heroin I would buy. The more heroin I snorted, the worse my skin would get, and the more stressed I would become. I couldn't find the source of my sadness, my stress, or my acne. Each thing was feeding the other things.

Through childhood and my teens, my skin was clear. I didn't have a blemish. I was like Snow White: pale, with soft skin and a round face. My best friend K had the same complexion as me. "Ghosts!" the boys would call as we walked by. We covered up our insecurities with red lipstick and Sun-In. We went tanning after school every day. My skin was fake-baked and glowing into my late teens. We didn't know how lucky we were that acne products weren't part of our regime. I didn't have Noxema or Pro-active or Retin-A because I did not need them. Until I did.

I moved to New York City at twenty—acne-free, but with insecurities intact. K went away to college. Around twenty-two or twenty-three, I started having benign breakouts. I thought it was a fluke. I thought that I was having a weird week. Then I thought I was having a weird couple months. I went into denial. I wasn't going to have a problem with acne because I wasn't a person who got acne.

I've used drugs to numb myself since I was sixteen. They've helped me be there but not really *there*. When my parents separated, I smoked pot four times a day. When the man I loved didn't love me back, I drank myself silly and snorted cocaine. After my car accident, I fell into the painkiller vortex. And most recently, heroin (and other opiates) helped me cope with my acne problem. Got a bunch of zits? Buy a bag of heroin. Depressed about how you look? Text your drug dealer. What else was there to do?

I read a comment on xoJane once: "Fuck acne! It's evil. It has literally made me forget who I am as a person." I get it.

After years of roaming and railing, at twenty-five, face in an uproar, I began living with my dad in upstate New York. He stood in line at CVS with me after my first dermatologist appointment. I cried. My prescription for Differin was something like 175 dollars. My dad looked scared of my sadness. We went out to breakfast carrying the prescription bags of expensive acne products that wouldn't work. The place was French, called Le Gamin. There were mirrors on the walls. I sat in the booth, facing away from the mirror. My dad pointed them out. "I know," I said. "Why do you think I'm sitting on this side?"

I would not have chosen to have my heroin phase take place while I was living under my father's roof, but we don't always decide when certain drugs come into our life. The thing about my heroin experience is that I did heroin when I did the most mundane things. I snorted heroin and went to the Dollar General. I went to Stop & Shop and bought yogurt. I treated my acne. I changed my profile picture. I cleaned my room. I went to bed. I wasn't out partying. I was home in bed on the computer reading acne forums. When you stay in your bedroom and have heroin, you're a king. You can be a king while eating an apple.

K graduated college by a thread and moved to the city where I lived. We've known each other since age seven—since we swam in the river behind her house and got snake bites. She's always been the closest thing to a sister I'll ever have. The kind of friend with whom you immediately launch into the important stuff: who you've slept with, how you feel, what mental illness you think you have. "If I have it, *you* have it!" we liked to yell at each other. "Oh, *I* don't have it," the other would say with a smile. Later, after some drinks or that night's drug of choice, we'd come around. "You were right before. I *have* always thought I had histrionic Borderline Personality Disorder."

Even our acne overlapped. While she was in college and I was in various cities, her text messages to me consisted of miserable photos of her face. And we texted products back and forth—so hopeful that we'd finally found the answer. "You gotta buy this!" we'd text, with a photo of tea-tree soap or Dr. Bronners or whatever.

K understood when I cried about my skin, and she would hug me through the window of the car and say, "I know, I know. Lie in the sun. Take a shower. Don't pick at it. Here, have the rest of my heroin." She understood.

Our relationship was precarious, dangerous even. My mother thought she was a bad influence on me, and her mother thought I was a bad influence on her. We'd begin the evening by walking around in the sun, complaining about how small our town was. Then we'd go for a beer. Then tequila shots. We waited for the other to say, "We should get shit. We should text B." One of us always said it. The other always agreed. We enabled each other. We wanted each other to feel good. We stayed out all night talking about monogamy, men, women, mothers. Did we want to have children? Did we want to get clean? We got riled up. We cried and laughed uncontrollably. And we went to the bathroom to do lines together. K usually puked. She had a weak stomach.

In the afternoon, she'd call me around three after she'd woken up. We giggled and giggled into the phone about our antics. No words needed to be spoken.

My acne was so bad I couldn't sleep on one side of my face. I couldn't smile or chew. I couldn't go to *work*. I couldn't see myself. Acne makes you feel desperate. Heroin makes you feel beautiful. They went hand in hand. Heroin helped me survive.

At my best, I'd have a day or two of clear-ish skin. Once I was lucky enough for this to coincide with the day I had to do a reading in New York City. Like an alcoholic, I didn't only do heroin when I was down. I did it when I was up. That morning I took the Amtrak two hours to the city, I bought three decks of heroin and shoved them in my jeans. I did some in the train bathroom. As the train pulled into Penn Station, my phone vibrated. It was my ex. The one it took me three years and three cities to let go of. He was saying hi. Letting me know that he'd love to see me if I ever came to the city.

Obviously, I could have ignored it. But he caught me on a clear-skin-and-heroin-possession day. I could hang out with him but have my secret friend, my scapegoat, my false confidence. I pondered this. I went into Urban Outfitters. I was also having a good body-image day. I tried on some sexy dresses. It was June in Manhattan and it was hot. I bought a bright blue sundress with spaghetti straps that showed off my cleavage nicely. I poured some heroin out of the baggie onto my cell phone in the dressing room, looking myself in the eye, smiling. Then I texted him back. "I'm actually here now. Do you want to meet me at the Strand?"

We met up and sat in Union Square. We had drinks at a bar we'd never been to before. It was too early and hot for red wine, but I loved it with heroin, so I got a glass anyway. I went to the bathroom twice to snort more. I was honest with him about my struggles. I alluded to the fact that I'd been partying pretty hard. He said, "Well, you don't look like it. You look really good. Healthy." And there it was—the ability to appear one thing and to be another.

The night went like this: bar after bar, me getting more and more high. Never one to keep much to myself, when we got to his apartment, I came clean. His response: "Can I do a line?"

We had sloppy sex all night—neither of us could come. I remember brushing my hair a lot because it felt really good. In the morning, I had to sneakily get up early to put make-up on so he wouldn't see my real face. We got bagels, hung out on the roof of a building and talked. He told me he didn't like heroin. He liked coke better. I left for my train and headed back upstate, riding high on anxiety. The next day, I broke out with cysts all over my face. "Why do we do these things?" I asked a friend. "Why do we go backward?" "We do them to remember why we don't do them," he said.

I read an article called "Why Acne Psychologist Ted Grossbart Blames My Ex for My Bad Skin." He says: "Your skin, as a loyal part of your mind/body complex, may well be saying, Hey, we need to protect her from getting hurt."

"Do you ever think that you and K have bad skin now

because of … karma?" my friend Amy asked me. She had a point. K and I were bitches in high school.

Buddhists say that anger causes acne. And I was angry—angry at myself. Where was my character? Where was my discipline? Where *was* I? Wasn't I better than this? And yet, I could not stop. I dreaded when my dad would have me go do an errand—because each time I got into the PT Cruiser, I'd drive to my dealer's block. "Hey," I'd text. "Hey girl, how many slices?" he'd ask. My usual was two. They were tiny wax bags, with a red or black stamp on them. They had different names. "Fire" was one. "Apple" was another. And then—I kid you not—there was "Soul Killer."

Was it anger or was it my karma? Was it my hormones or was it my genes? Should I cut out meat or should I cut out dairy? Was I allergic to gluten? Was it my ex or was it my stress level? No one knew. And yet everyone had an opinion. I was enraged, frustrated, mortified, and heartbroken.

"I want to *kill someone*!" was my mantra. That was my thing to yell. "I want to *kill someone*." Such terrible words to utter. "I don't think you want to kill someone," my dad tried to reason with me. "I do! I do, Dad! I really would love to. I want to *kill someone*." On that morning, I slammed my fist into the wall like a fourteen-year-old boy. My father was shocked, as was I.

But I wasn't in control of myself anymore. I stomped into the bathroom and slammed the door behind me.

I stepped into the dreaded shower. I hated taking showers and using my dumb products that weren't working, I hated feeling the bumps on my face, but I mostly hated stepping out and having to look at myself in the mirror with no make-up on. And putting make-up on sucked, too. Mornings were the worst. I looked like I had been hit by a truck. It took me forever to make myself look even a little less dead. My dad kept telling me that he wished he could take it on for me, that he would if he could. It choked me up whenever he said this. I wished he could, too.

An essay about cystic acne read: "Fighting acne is like fighting a war. There is collateral damage. Things get worse before they get better."

Things got worse. At my lowest, I was my highest. In early December, me, K and another friend drove to New York City. I was battling a stubborn cyst on the side of my face but, besides that, my skin was decent. I gave a reading at Happy Ending Lounge on Bowery Street. I'd invited my friend J, a functioning heroin addict. He slipped me two hot pink baggies. K and I went into the bathroom. And we came out way happier. This was nothing like the stuff we got from my dealer. This was the real deal. We had grand fun that night—that much I know—but I don't remember much. Only that I *felt* good.

Our friend dropped K and me off at my house at 4 a.m. We went into my room, fell into bed and snuggled into each other.

Around 5:30 a.m., K and I both jumped up—like we heard it at the same time. It was my father on the phone. He was talking about us. He was defending us. Defending me. He was saying I wasn't doing drugs. K and I got out of bed and put our ears to the door. We looked at each other with shocked eyes. Eventually we opened the door.

My dad hung up. He was pissed. Not at us. At the person on the phone. K's mom. She was onto us.

I haven't mentioned this yet, but K's boyfriend was a cop. She lived with him, and he had found an empty heroin wrapper. He called K's mom, who then called my dad. K and I sat on the wooden floor outside of my room wearing boxers, T-shirts, and our make-up from the night before. I felt about twelve years old.

My father—my fiercely loyal father—was kind but stern. He said, "But if you're doing heroin, I want you to *cut the shit*. I have a short rope for that. My brother died from it."

"We're not!" we told him. "We're not."

I remembered my father's brother. Uncle Steve. He was my favorite uncle as a kid. He was always in a reclined chair, dozing off. He ate CoCo Puffs and drank Sunny D. He was laid-back and there, but not really *there*. I was with my father at Uncle Steve's funeral. I was twelve. I'd never seen my dad cry before. I lay my head on his shoulder. I always told my dad that Uncle Steve reminded me of Will Smith's character in *The Fresh Prince of Bel-Air*. My dad loved that story—often asked me to repeat it.

I wondered if my father 100 percent believed K and me. I really just wished someone would ask me if I was OK so that I could say no. Even *I* could see that my behavior was erratic. I was either sleeping ten hours a night or not sleeping at all. I was either binge eating or not eating at all. The sky was always falling. I was always pissed about something. Everyone was an asshole. Everything was annoying. When I woke up in the mornings, I would find that I wrote things online that I did not remember. I sent naked photographs of myself to people, and then I would forget. My wallet was chock-full of empty heroin wrappers. I flushed them down the toilet when I remembered, but usually I forgot to. I wasn't exactly organized. Sometimes, when I was paying for gas or gum or something, I'd reach into the change pocket and feel all of the little baggies, reminding me of my other self.

During my workdays, I watched videos of Cassandra Bankson to comfort myself. Cassandra Bankson is a model who, like me, had severe cystic acne. On her YouTube channel, she posts videos of herself and her acne struggles. Sometimes my dad watched them with me. She made one video that she begins with make-up on, then she washes it off. She says, "This is my biggest insecurity." She showed her acne to the camera. It's absolutely amazing, and it's the only thing in the world like itself. One night when my cousin was visiting, we stayed up past midnight in my bed watching videos of her. I couldn't believe what my life had turned into.

There were only certain foods I was eating—mainly Dannon Light and Fit Pineapple Coconut yogurt. You could pretty much taste the chemicals in it; there must have been something really, *really* bad for you in it. I craved milk and dairy. I became tiny. I was in my sixteen-year-old body. "You gonna eat something?" my dad started saying to me. "I bet you weigh what you weighed in high school," K said one night when we were hanging out in my room trying on dresses. "You look like a completely different person from the back," she said.

Throughout all of this, I was still going to yoga. Even after doing heroin all day. Once I was heaving into the toilet, but I shoved a piece of bread in my mouth and ran across the street to yoga. Yoga feels good. Heroin feels good. Together they felt like heaven.

Sometimes, in between everything, I'd have revelatory days. Days when I'd had enough of my pathetic self-destruction. On those days, I read *When Things Fall Apart* by Pema Chödrön and drank Smooth Move, trying to get all the toxins out of my body. I underlined sentences in the book that were meaningful to me. This was great for a few hours, and then I'd buckle and text my dealer, praying he wouldn't answer. Heroin is exactly the opposite of being in the present moment. I needed to spend twenty dollars on some light-brown powder to put up my nose to be in the present moment. Being in the present moment cost me.

I went from denying I had bad skin and avoiding the topic, to it being all I talked about. I couldn't have a conversation without bringing it up. "What's wrong?" someone would ask. "My skin. My skin. My skin." I was obsessed. I tried everything for my acne. I tried the hard stuff: Benzoyl Peroxide, Pro-active, and topicals like Differin and Duac gel. I tried antibiotics: Doxycycline, Minocycline, and Oracea. I tried tea: green, nettle, skin detox, healthy fasting, valerian root. I tried vitamins: milk thistle; hair, skin and nails; zinc. I tried restorative yoga, acupuncture, even lavender oil on my forehead. I tried meditating on having clear skin. I changed my pillowcases each night. I refused to take Accutane because someday I want to have a baby. At the end of my rope, I tried ortho-tri-cyclen, which turned me into a suicidal, emotional mess and gave me the "initial break-out," which was hell on earth. When nothing worked, I just didn't leave my house. I cried in my dad's arms on the couch. I was even embarrassed to meet my dealer. I kept my hair in front of my face and wore big, unflattering sunglasses.

And then the heroin stopped working. I told this to my friend, a recovering drug addict, and he said, "You could probably just eat dark chocolate at this point, and it would do the same thing." My tolerance was high. So was K's. We yelled at the dealer, telling him he was selling us shit. We bought Suboxen and started to wean off. We ordered these herb capsules called Kratom that are supposed to make you feel good, and we popped them and pretended they worked. We walked around and drank cherry slushies and ate candy. The only other option, if we wanted the heroin to feel good again, was to shoot it. And I wasn't going to do that, though I'd be a liar if I said I didn't entertain the idea.

One of my yoga teachers used to say that what is nectar for you in the beginning is poison in the long run, and what feels like poison in the beginning is nectar in the end. It annoyed me how often he said this because it resonated with me so much. "Shut up!" I thought. "I know. I know."

I don't live in the same city anymore. I'm in therapy and my therapist says it's going to take a while for me to piece myself back together.

It's early January, and I haven't had a pedicure since August. My feet look dry and sad, but my face, finally, looks alive.

Four Lessons in Being Human

By Peter Brown Hoffmeister

1.

My friend is doing Sensory Deprivation Floatation Tank sessions. I ask him to explain.

He says, "I pay $60 to float for 90 minutes. I get in something sorta like a coffin that's filled with 94-degree saltwater."

"Wait, you get in a coffin?"

"*Like* a coffin," he says. "The goal is to float successfully."

"How does one float successfully?"

"Well, you get into a lucid dreaming state."

I have to look this thing up. And there are some sketchy sites on the topic. But there is also a *Wall Street Journal* article, and one on *Slate*. So I read those. And according to *Slate*, floating is a "profound, ecstatic state of nothingness…achieved while floating naked in a sensory deprivation tank." According to the Gravity Spa website, floating can help the brain "access the mysterious, elusive state of theta wave production."

But I get stuck on words like "naked," so I ask my friend again. "So people float naked?"

He says, "The first time was crazy. I had a dream about owls, man."

"Cool," I say, "but let me get this straight: you pay $60 to get in a coffin half-filled with saltwater. And you're naked."

"Yep, then they close the lid, and you don't know where you are. Total sensory deprivation."

"Awesome," I say, "and you dream?"

"Well, if you float successfully, you dream."

"So, is floating successfully just a euphemism for sleeping? Are you paying $60 for a 90-minute nap?"

"No, no, man. Clearly you don't understand."

Clearly.

I tell my friend Corrina about the naked floating and she says, "That sounds a little hipster. Do all the people who work at the floating tanks have mustaches?"

"Probably," I say.

"You'd have to pay me to get into someone else's warm naked tank. You know people jack off in there."

Clearly, she doesn't understand either.

2.

On June 18th, 2000, anarchists from around the country organized in my hometown of Eugene, Oregon to mark the one-year anniversary of an anarchist riot. Four hundred protesters gathered in a park and smashed a dummy of a police officer using potatoes, skateboards, and boots. Speakers called for an end to capitalism. A dozen anarchists used puppets to reenact police violence, while 80 others marched into downtown. It was very well organized.

On 7th street, the anarchists gathered in front of the federal building and threw batteries against the windows, chanting "Red Rover, Red Rover, send fascists right over," hoping for a senator or a congressman to exit the building. But the politicians weren't coming forward, and riot police had locked down the building ahead of time. A S.W.A.T. team was in the lobby, waiting for the command to arrest the anarchists (which they eventually did).

I was working in the lobby of that federal building, selling coffee and baked goods, when the riot took place. I found it funny that anarchists, who were chanting slogans against organization, had organized these events. I also thought it was funny that they performed a puppet show. I asked, "Do anarchists enjoy puppet shows?"

My friend said, "The puppets depict the fascists, man."

"Oh," I said.

"Yeah, man," my friend said. "Fuck the police, you know?"

"Okay," I said, "but the anarchists have leadership and organization and all that. Isn't that hilarious?"

"Why?" he said, "Are you, a fascist, Pete?"

"Yes," I said. "I'm a fascist."

3.

Like I said, during that anarchists' riot I was working at the coffee shop on the ground floor of the federal building. I was in there when the S.W.A.T. team locked it down, put zip-ties on the insides of the doors, announced that no one was going in or out, and sent a runner up to the political offices on the upper floors.

I called my manager and asked her if she wanted me to close the café down.

She said, "Maybe keep it open for a while and see if the cops end up buying anything."

So I left the café open. And the cops did purchase goods. They bought doughnuts, all of the fresh doughnuts. Then they started buying the day-old doughnuts, one by one. A cop would saunter over to the counter with his riot gear on, look at the display case as if he was considering what to buy, then go ahead and buy another doughnut. When I was down to my last day-old doughnut, one of the S.W.A.T guys walked up with his helmet tipped back, his AR-15 rifle slung across the front of his Kevlar vest.

He pointed to the last doughnut, a crusty little old-fashioned circle that had been there since yesterday morning. As if he were truly considering its merits, he said, "I think I'll take that one right there."

"That's the last day-old doughnut." I said. "You guys ate all of the doughnuts."

"Yep," he said.

"Isn't that funny?" I said.

The cop tilted his head to the side like he didn't understand what I was saying. "Why?" he said.

4.

For the following anecdote to make sense, you have to understand that I am not a tall man. I am, as my students say, "a fun-sized person."

My sophomore year in college, when I was on the wrestling team, the program guide listed my height as 5'6". I was elated. That is, by far, the tallest height anyone has ever given me. In all honesty, if I woke up in the morning (when humans are the tallest), and went directly to an anti-gravity bar to hang for ten minutes, I still wouldn't be 5'6".

People have made fun of me for my height, or lack thereof, my entire life. I'm not complaining; it's just a fact. And I usually don't mind too much. I'm not a big man. I'm okay with that.

Do I sound defensive?

Anyway, I was in the store the other day, in the dairy section, where all of the butter, yogurt, and milk are housed. At our local grocery market, this is sort of an enclosed space. We get in each other's way back there, do a lot of excuse-mes and oh-sorrys.

So I walked into that small dairy section, and I hear a kid's voice. "Thomas, Thomas, look! There's a midget!"

I looked at the kid tapping his brother's shoulder. They were both grade-school-aged, youngish kids, both really excited.

Then I looked around the milk section trying to figure out where the midget was. Even though I'm a small man and naturally tend to defend little people, I like seeing midgets too. So I looked behind the butter fridge, looked out past the orange juice, past the yogurt, past the chocolate milk. But I didn't see the midget. In fact, I didn't see anyone. I was alone in the dairy section.

I looked back at the boys. They were both staring at me.

"Thomas," the first one whispered, "look, it's a midget." He pointed.

I just stood there next to the butter.

Then their mother walked up. Apparently she'd heard the kid yelling about me being a midget and she was here to correct the misconception.

I thought she was going to say, "Oh, no, son, that's not a midget. That's a smallish, full-size man." Or something like that.

But instead, she said, "Sweetie, you've got to be quieter. They can hear you when you talk about them."

Curandera

By Caroline Paul

The first thing that happened was I hit an engine block. It wasn't supposed to be there, in the middle lane of the freeway, me going 75 and not seeing it until the car in front of me swerved and a piece of rubber from the tire spit into the sky. There was little to do but grip the steering wheel, inhale, drive into it.

I felt the thud as the bumper knocked it over. I heard the sickening scrape. But the car was upright, driving forward. The errant engine block had fit under the chassis, barely.

A closer inspection showed a ripped underbelly; the car flayed like a fish, one metal shard just millimeters from my gas tank. My mechanic's voice was tight as she explained the disaster so nearly averted: the metal piercing a hole in the tank, an errant spark, and Poof.

A week later my surfboard flipped out from under me on a baby wave and hit me in the face. "You almost shattered your eyeball socket," said the emergency room doctor, and called in a plastic surgeon.

It continued like this for the next few months, a series of small disasters that seemed independent of my free will. I began to look around me when I stepped out of the house. I jumped at sudden noises. I had never been particularly superstitious, but now I wondered if there was such thing as luck, and whether mine had run out.

But luck was too benign, and random. This felt intentional. And bigger, much bigger. I told my friends I had a funny feeling that the universe was out to get me. "Can't you see?" I whined. "The cosmos is a mugger. Turn a corner and there it is, wielding a gun, demanding your money."

Some friends laughed, others nodded and put a hand on my shoulder. My girlfriend and I had broken up in the late summer. I had suffered doubt and the required bouts of self-loathing, they knew, and these strange mutterings were probably just another side effect.

I hurt my knee. I got the flu.

'I think you've been cursed," a friend finally said to me. She explained: the same thing had happened to her. She had been working in Cuba. She was robbed twice in a few days, and her film camera had unexpectedly broken. The locals said she was cursed. They advised her to get un-cursed quickly.

"You need to go to a curandera, like I did," she told me.

I didn't know what a curandera was.

"Shaman. Healer. Witch doctor. You get the picture," my friend replied.

Let me tell you, a curandera is not so easy to find. A Yelp search yielded little. But someone knew someone who knew someone and finally, a four-block area was narrowed down. I bet on the shop with the window full of candles, and crosses and jars of herbs, and walked inside. It was dark. The air smelled of vanilla and dust. Customers wafted about like specters. My heart was woo-woo Californian, but my brain was WASPy Connecticut, and it now whispered, "Why are you here?" I wasn't sure. Part of me wanted to step back into what I understood. But another part—the desperate part—knew that this mysterious world of spirits held hope. Around me women put candles into shopping bags. Men peered at saint medallions and zippo lighters.

The shop owner looked more like a school principal than

a witch doctor. We sat at a rickety linoleum table, and she sized me up.

"So," she said, her tone brusque, one eyebrow raised, as if she already knew my problems were cosmic small potatoes, and her Wiccan duties were needed elsewhere. But she listened as I explained, and then told me that she, and the spirit Esmeralda, could help. She shook a palmful of seashells like dice. She said some incantations: "Esmeralda, Esmeralda" was what I caught.

With a flick of the wrist, the shells clattered onto the table then came to rest; she stared at them, murmured again. Suddenly I felt calmer than I had in months. Perhaps because I was finally taking control of my predicament. Perhaps it felt good to consult mysterious forces similar to the ones that seemed to be pursuing me. The curandera looked up from the shells.

"You haven't been cursed," she told me. "But there has been a spell."

This, she said, was a relief. A curse is direct, powerful, thrown specifically at you, she explained. A spell is more diffuse—negative energy someone feels toward you—with no direct intent to harm. But this still felt ominous. Who felt negative energy toward me? Even my ex-girlfriend seemed unlikely—

we may have been ill-suited but we were not malicious.

The curandera didn't seem to care who did what; the spell just needed to be broken. She and the spirit Esmeralda again consulted. More whispers, more closed eyes. Prayers, and pointing in my direction. I was handed a Virgin Mary candle and a large plastic bottle, and though the cap read 7UP, the curandera told me it held flowered water. The candle was to be kept lit for three days. I was to pour the flowered water over me during my next shower.

I took my candle and my soda jug of flower water home. I didn't doubt the power of Esmeralda as much as I doubted the spell part. I was sure no one disliked me enough to think bad thoughts. I didn't have enemies, didn't inspire envy. But I was tired of feeling vulnerable. I was tired of wondering when the next accident would happen. Fussing more than necessary, I found a place for the candle on the mantle. I took my flower water shower. Then I walked around the house in careful, mincing steps, in case I had simply angered the forces against me.

A few hours later the phone rang; it was my credit union. "For the past few weeks someone's been in your account," the clerk told me. "But we caught the perpetrators today, so it won't happen again, and you'll be fully reimbursed."

I stood still, clutching the phone, staring at the candle. I knew then that the spell had been broken.

And it was true. Weeks passed. No weird mishaps, no crazy misadventures. I began to relax, and see the universe as benevolent again. But still I wondered, who would put a spell on me? Who had such disgust and dislike?

It took months, but one day I realized who the perp was.

It was me. Don't we hate ourselves after a breakup? We look in the mirror and see someone unlovable. We loop the fights we started, the nasty things we said, the love we should have given. We can't believe we stayed that long. We lurch through the final fight and for the next year wander around stunned, stopping only to writhe in self-pity and loathing. We commit unconscious self-sabotage.

We put spells on ourselves.

So be generous with the you that is flawed and helpless. Be kind to the parts that are wounded, defensive, temporarily insane. But if pianos start falling from top floor buildings, or cliff edges crumble when you walk near, call upon your curandera and her spirit sidekick. Wash yourself clean, of yourself.

How to Feel Better About Falling Apart

By Mary Roach

Who said, "Middle age is the heinous and insidious conglomeration of small physical failings and defects that appear without warning and totally ruin your day"? It might have been me. I used to feel this way. But I have worked hard to develop a new and positive outlook about these things, which I will now share with you, so you will feel better too.

Unpigmented white spots on forearms. Compared with those little red, raised blobs on your chest and upper arms, these white spots are hardly noticeable. By the way, I'm guessing they're not only on your arms. Have you examined the fronts of your shins lately?

Red blobs on chest. These are barely visible from across

a large, poorly lit room. Try to associate with people with limited vision.

Receding gums. What you are failing to realize is that the enamel underneath your gums has been protected from unsightly coffee and cigarette stains for the past thirty years and is as white and perfect as your toilet bowl above the waterline. Also, many of you have the problem of unflattering gummy smiles, and this will be alleviated by the gradual disappearance of your gums.

Crow's feet. If you've ever examined the foot of a crow up close, you'll see that the lines around your eyes, while they detract from your once-youthful looks and tend to act as foundation sinks, are not as ugly as the actual foot of a crow.

Unsightly neck cords coming down from jaw. These can easily be taken care of by cultivating a double chin. Don't want a double chin? Well today's your lucky day, because you don't have one!

Liver spots. They call them liver spots because you've lived a lot. You're a liver. If you'd done less of that living out in the sun without the good sense to put on sunscreen, you'd be a liver without spots, but never mind, too late for that now.

Yellowing toenails. Why is red a desirable toenail color and yellow not? True fact: There are yellow nail polishes one can buy, though only the young have the poor sense to do this. Did you know that this condition is caused by a living fungus in your toenails? Take solace in knowing you are providing safe harbor for one of God's small creatures.

Saggy folds in flesh above the knee. When was the last time someone complimented your knees? No one cares about your knees. If your ass is holding up and your breasts are still above your navel, you have no place carping about your knees.

Loose, flappy skin on underside of forearm. You probably haven't noticed this one. Look in the mirror while crossing your arms. See what I'm talking about? Remember, until ten seconds ago, you didn't care about this. Why care now?

Unwanted hairs. Georgia O'Keeffe had visible wiry chin hairs, but no one remembers her for this. They remember her for large, vaginal nature paintings. Let this be an inspiration.

Vertical wrinkles growing from upper lip. Don't trouble yourself over these, because soon there will be large heavy folds on either side of your mouth, and when this happens, you'll give anything to go back to the days when you only worried about upper lip lines. And you know what? You're living those glorious halcyon days right now!

Heavy, dark under-eye circles. Many athletes apply black greasepaint to this area to reduce glare and improve their game.

You don't ever have to do this. That's a savings right there.

Skin tags. If you look through a dermatology textbook, you'll see that some people have even uglier things growing out of their skin. I heard somewhere that they don't necessarily all get bigger and bigger.

Gray hairs. Hairs coarsen and crook when they go gray. While some people feel that the frazzled, even witchlike appearance of gray hair is unattractive, those of you who have lived your whole life with thin, limp, Tom Petty hair will probably enjoy the added body.

Bulldog jowls. Don't let heavy jowls get you down. You know why? Because then you won't smile, and when you smile, no one can tell you have jowls.

Creases in front of ears. Police investigators use these to gauge perpetrators' ages in cases where it's hard to tell. Think of them like fingerprints. They make you you. Though if you've got neck cords, receding gums, skin tags and bulldog jowls, God knows no one needs ear creases to tell your age.

I hope that you feel better now.

Contributors

Chloe Caldwell is the author of the essay collection *Legs Get Led Astray* and the novella, *Women*. Her work has appeared in *Salon.com*, *The Sun*, *Nylon*, *Men's Health*, *The Rumpus*, and the anthologies *True Tales of Lust and Love*, and *Goodbye To All That: Writers on Loving and Leaving NYC*. She lives in Hudson, New York **chloecaldwell.com**

Novella Carpenter is the author of *Farm City: The Education of an Urban Farmer*. Her latest book is *Gone Feral: Tracking My Dad Through the Wild* (2014). She runs Ghost Town Farm from the formerly vacant lot at the side of her Oakland, CA home. She has taught writing at the California College of the Arts and now teaches full-time at the University of San Francisco.

Chris Colin is the author most recently of *What to Talk About*, as well as *What Really Happened to the Class of '93* and *Blindsight*, named one of Amazon's best books of 2011. He's written about chimp filmmakers, ethnic cleansing, George Bush's pool boy, blind visual artists and more for the *NewYorker.com*, *The New York Times Magazine*, *Pop-Up Magazine*, *Wired*, *Mother Jones*, *McSweeney's* and *Afar*, where he's a contributing writer. He lives in San Francisco. **chriscolin.com**

Meghan Daum's latest book is *The Unspeakable: And Other Subjects of Discussion*. She is also the author of three other books as well as the editor of *Selfish, Shallow & Self-Absorbed: Sixteen Writers on the*

*Decision Not to Have Kid*s. Meghan has been an opinion columnist at *The Los Angeles Times* for nearly a decade and has written for numerous magazines, including *The New Yorker*, *The New York Times Magazine*, *Harper's*, and *Vogue*. **meghandaum.com**

Brian Doyle is the author of the sprawling Oregon novel *Mink River* and the headlong sea novel *The Plover*. His newest book is the novel *Martin Marten*, set on Oregon's Mount Hood. Among various honors for his work are a Catholic Book Award, three Pushcart Prizes, the John Burroughs Award for Nature Essays, the *Foreword Reviews* Book of the Year Award in 2011, and, puzzling him to this day, the 2008 Award in Literature from the American Academy of Arts and Letters. Brian Doyle edits *Portland Magazine* at the University of Portland in Oregon.

Susan Gregg Gilmore is the bestselling author of three novels including *Looking For Salvation at the Dairy Queen* and *The Improper Life of Bezellia Grove*. Her most recent work, *The Funeral Dress*, was called a "revelatory novel that offers an evocative account of the lives of Appalachian working women" (*Kirkus Review*). It was a TARGET Emerging Author Selection and a TARGET Recommended Read. Gilmore has written for publications including the *Los Angeles Times*, *Christian Science Monitor*, and *Garden & Gun*. She lives in Chattanooga with her husband and three dogs. **susangreggilmore.com**

Peter Brown Hoffmeister is the author of three books, *The End of Boys*, *Let Them Be Eaten by Bears*, and *Graphic the Valley*, and his next two novels are forthcoming from Knopf. His favorite independent bookstores are Tsunami Books in Eugene, Oregon; Powell's Books in Portland; and Books Inc. in California. **peterbrownhoffmeister.com**

Anne Lamott is the author of seven novels including *Hard Laughter*, *Rosie*, and *Imperfect Birds*. She has also written several bestselling memoirs including *Operating Instructions*, an account of life as a single mother during her son's first year, followed by *Some Assembly Required: A Journal of My Son's First Son*, and a writing guide titled *Bird by Bird: Some Instructions on Writing and Life*. Her collections of autobiographical essays on faith include *Traveling Mercies: Some Thoughts on Faith*, *Grace (Eventually): Thoughts on Faith*, and *Help, Thanks, Wow: The Three Essential Prayers*. Her new book of essays is called *Small Victories: Spotting Improbable Moments of Grace*.

Rachel Levin is a San Francisco-based journalist who has written for the *New Yorker*, *The New York Times*, *Outside*, and *Sunset*, where she was a senior travel editor. A member of the San Francisco Writers' Grotto, she has contributed to *Pop-Up* magazine and *Best Food Writing* and is a contributing editor at OZY Media. **byrachellevin.com**

Yiyun Li grew up in Beijing and came to the United States in 1996. Her debut collection, *A Thousand Years of Good Prayers*, won the Frank O'Connor International Short Story Award, PEN/Hemingway Award, Guardian First Book Award, and California Book Award for first fiction. She is the author of the novel, *The Vagrants*, which won the gold medal of California Book Award for fiction; the story collection *Gold Boy, Emerald Girl*, a finalist of Story Prize; and *Kinder Than Solitude*, her latest novel, published to critical acclaim. Her books have been translated into more than twenty languages. She teaches at the University of California, Davis. **yiyunli.com**

Kathryn Ma is the author of the novel *The Year She Left Us*, named a *New York Times* Editor's Choice and an NPR Best Book of the Year. Her story collection, *All That Work and Still No Boys*, won the Iowa Short Fiction Award. She received the Meyerson Prize for Fiction and has published her short fiction widely. **kathrynma.com**

Scott McClanahan is the writer of *Crapalachia* and *Hill William*. He lives in West Virginia and makes music with Holler Boys. **hollerpresents.com**

Janis Cooke Newman is the author of the memoir *The Russian Word for Snow*, the novel *Mary*, and the forthcoming novel, *A Master Plan for Rescue*. She is the founder of the Lit Camp writers conference. **janiscookenewman.com**

It is no surprise that in 2010, *The New York Times Magazine* featured **James Patterson** on its cover and hailed him as having "transformed book publishing," and that *Time* magazine hailed him as "The Man Who Can't Miss." In 2011, it was estimated that one-in-four of all hardcover suspense/thriller novels sold were written by James Patterson. He holds the Guinness record for the most #1 *New York Times* bestsellers of any author. He is a tireless advocate for literacy, books, bookstores, and getting kids hooked on reading. **jamespatterson.com**

Caroline Paul is a native New Englander and an identical twin. She wrote about her thirteen-and-a-half year career as a San Francisco firefighter in *Fighting Fire*, an updated version of which came out in 2011. She is also the author of the novel *East Wind, Rain*. A movie based on the book is in production. Her third book *Lost Cat, A True Story of Love, Desperation and GPS Technology* was named a Best Book by Jezebel and by the influential website Brainpickings. It has also been optioned for a film. **carolinepaul.com**

Michelle Richmond is the author of six books, including the international bestseller *The Year of Fog*. Her latest novel, *Golden State*, imagines modern-day California on the brink of secession from the nation, and her latest story collection, *Hum*, won the Catherine Doctorow Innovative Fiction Prize. She is the publisher of Fiction Attic Press. **michellerichmond.com**

Journalist, humorist, and science writer **Mary Roach** is the author most recently of *Gulp: Adventures on the Alimentary Canal*. Her previous books include *Stiff*, *Spook*, and *Packing for Mars*. She lives in the Bay Area and has no hobbies. **maryroach.net**

Lavinia Spalding is a writer, editor, teacher, public speaker, and lapsed Luddite. She's series editor of *The Best Women's Travel Writing*, and the author of two books: *Writing Away: A Creative Guide to Awakening the Journal-Writing Traveler*, and *With a Measure of Grace, the Story and Recipes of a Small Town Restaurant*. Lavinia's work has appeared in many print and online publications, including *Yoga Journal*, *Sunset* magazine, *The Guardian UK*, *Tin House*, Lonely Planet's *An Innocent Abroad*, and *The Best Travel Writing*, volumes 9 and 10. She lives in San Francisco, where she's a resident of the Writers' Grotto. **laviniaspalding.com**

Wendy Spero is the author of *Microthrills: True Stories from a Life of Small Highs*. Her writing has appeared in various publications, including *The New York Times*, *New York Times Magazine* and *Esquire*. As a performer, she has been featured on The Moth, NPR and Comedy Central's *Premium Blend*. Her latest one woman show, *Whose Your Daddy?* headlined at the Edinburgh Fringe Festival. **wendyspero.com**

Bonnie Tsui is a writer for *The New York Times*, *The Atlantic*, and *Pacific Standard*, and the author of *American Chinatown*. She is working on a new book about swimming. **bonnietsui.com**

Editor's bio

Samantha Schoech is the co-editor with Lisa Taggart of two previous anthologies including the bestselling *The Bigger the Better, The Tighter the Sweater: 21 Funny Women on Beauty, Body Image and Other Hazards of Being Female*. Her essays and fiction have appeared in many places including *Seventeen*, *The Sun*, *Glimmer Train*, and the *New York Times*. She contributes with some regularity to OZY.com and is the Program Director for Independent Bookstore Day. She lives in California with her bookseller husband and their twins. **samanthaschoech.com**

Acknowledgments

Independent Bookstore Day would like to thank all the authors who generously donated the work herein to benefit indie bookstores and the book-loving public, as well as everyone who worked to make this book a real, actual book: Christy Hale for her design prowess, Melita Granger for her eagle-eyed copyediting, and R. Black for the better-than-we-could-have-hoped-for cover art and design. We are humbled by your talent and generosity.

CPSIA information can be obtained at www.ICGtesting.com
Printed in the USA
LVOW10s1149260315

432121LV00002B/2/P